SECRET PROJECTS OF THE LUFTWAFFE
BLOHM & VOSS
BV 155

DAN SHARP

TEMPEST
BOOKS

*For Ronnie Olsthoorn who
always believed in me.*

First published in Great Britain in 2019
by Tempest Books
an imprint of Mortons Books Ltd.
Media Centre
Morton Way
Horncastle LN9 6JR
www.mortonsbooks.co.uk

ISBN 978 1 911658 32 0

Typeset by ATG Media
Printed and bound in Great Britain

10 9 8 7 6 5 4 3 2 1

Contents

Chapter 1
Introduction

Following the surrender of German forces in Hamburg, northern Germany, at 1pm on May 3, 1945, the city was occupied by British troops. Nearly a month later, on Wednesday, May 30, a team of three intelligence officers from the Combined Intelligence Objectives Sub-committee set off from London on a mission to assess 39 'target' locations in the Bremen and Hamburg area thought to be of military and industrial interest.

Colonel W A Shuping, Lee Worley and Richard H Depew Jr, all employees of the Fairchild Engine & Aircraft Corporation in the US, were first flown to Venlo in the Netherlands where they obtained two Ford cars from the British Army with two Belgian Army privates as drivers. They eventually arrived in Bremen, Germany, on the evening of May 31, ready to begin their task.

After a week of touring targets connected to Focke-Wulf, Weser Flugzeugbau and Blohm & Voss in the Bremen area, and now with the assistance of British Flight Lieutenant E A Littlefield, attached to the 2nd Tactical Air Force, RAF, they moved on to Hamburg. Among the three targets visited during the first day in this area, June 9, was the Blohm & Voss experimental aircraft factory at Finkenwärder – actually an island on the river Elbe to the west of the city centre. This consisted of well-equipped engineering workshops, administrative buildings, laboratories and a large hangar.

Damage from bombing was minimal – although most windows had been shattered during the bombing of nearby submarine pens. The Americans were impressed to find examples of the huge BV 222 and BV 238 flying boats under construction, alongside BV 246 glide bombs and another aircraft about which Allied intelligence had, up to this point, known very little – the BV 155.

Shuping, Worley and Depew were able to track down several of the key people who worked on the BV 155, including Blohm & Voss chief designer Richard Vogt and his assistant Hermann Pohlmann, and interrogate them about it. According to their report:[1] "In 1943 Messerschmitt offered the German Air Ministry a high altitude fighter with a designation Me 155, but received no order. Later, B&V was furnished with a sketch of this Messerschmitt aircraft, but after study changed it completely in evolving the B&V 155.

"This aircraft is a single engine high altitude fighter with a design ceiling of 16,000m (52,480ft). The calculated speed at ceiling was 750km/h (470mph). The engine was a Daimler-Benz 603 U and exhaust pipes passed down each side of the fuselage and drove a 2-stage turbo supercharger made by Hirth of Stuttgart.

"The air from the 2-stage turbo supercharger passed through intercoolers to the engine driven supercharger and thence to the engine. In the 155 B seen by this team, these intercoolers were located one at each end of the centre section. In the later model, 155 C, of which we saw the mock-up, the intercooler was located under the fuselage beneath and to the rear of the engine. The cabin was pressurised to 7,000m. An ingenious inflated tube sealed the sliding hatch cover to maintain the cabin pressure.

"The length of the airplane was approximately 11m and the span approximately 19.5m, the span of the centre section being about 10m. Dr Vogt stated that he believed the wing of this aircraft was possibly the first German wing with laminar flow. Flaps of split types were used on the centre section. The centre section used a single box spar of welded steel construction (125,000psi normalised). The outer wing panels were of monospar construction.

"The range was about 3 hours. The armament consists of one 30mm cannon in fuselage, firing through propeller hub, plus two 20mm cannon located one in each side of the centre section. In the 155 C it was proposed to use one 30mm and four 20mm cannon.

"It has been stated by Dr Vogt that one B&V 155 airplane had been completed and flown away to another location, but was crashed in landing near Neuminster [Neumünster – about 60km directly north of Hamburg], whereupon it was removed to a Lufthansa field. The crash was attributed to failure of the retractable landing gear to extend.

"The second B&V 155 B fighter was nearly completed ready for final assembly and this aircraft and one spare engine, has been secured and tagged for evacuation to the UK by this team. Also, we have secured, packed and marked for shipment to the UK, all original drawings, stress data, wind tunnel data, static test data, what flight test data was available, parts list, etc. for this airplane."

On June 14 the Americans tagged up 29 separate component parts of the disassembled BV 155 V2, including the spare Daimler-Benz DB 603 U engine, plus 50 boxes of documents, and Littlefield arranged for their transportation back to Britain. They decided to leave behind a second BV 155 B fuselage still in its jig and 75% complete – presumably the third prototype – a tail wheel shock strut and fork for the 155 B, the welded structure and jig of a BV 155 C fuselage, outer wing panel jigs, a BV 155 C mock-up and a further five spare DB 603 U engines. And on June 18, 1945, the team returned to London.

ABOVE: British RAF Regiment soldiers hold up a captured model of the BV 155 B for the camera at Blohm & Voss's offices in Finkenwärder, Hamburg in June 1945. The photo was among several included in the CIOS XXV-53 German Aircraft Industry Bremen-Hamburg Area intelligence report by Fairchild employees Shuping, Worley and Depew.

ABOVE: Another image from CIOS XXV-53 taken inside a hangar at Finkenwärder showing a man posing with a captured BV 246 glide bomb. Most of the buildings at Finkenwärder had suffered damage as a result of heavy Allied bombing.

It was the end of a story which began three years earlier during the spring of 1942. At that time, following the German declaration of war on the USA, on December 11, 1941, the Luftwaffe and the Reichsluftfahrtministerium (RLM – the German Air Ministry) were considering what sort of weapons the Americans might employ in the European theatre and how they might combat them.

In particular, the Germans were aware that the USAAF had either ordered or intended to order a fleet of high-altitude bombers. Details were evidently scant on the precise performance of these aircraft but it was expected that they would be capable of operating well above 10km (32,800ft) and would make an appearance towards the end of 1942 at the earliest.

The first topic up for discussion at the GL-Besprechung or 'Generalluftzeugmeister meeting' – effectively a gathering of key decision-makers from within the RLM and the Luftwaffe – on May 12, 1942, was the Höhenjäger or 'high-altitude fighter'[2]. At the outset RLM engineer Flugbaumeister Walter Friebel stated that there were two options for this role: aircraft with piston engines and aircraft with jet engines but the second would not yet be discussed. He then read out a list of standard production fighter types "available in the period 1942/43" – the Messerschmitt Bf 109 F-4, Bf 109 G-1 and Me 309, Focke-Wulf Fw 190 A-3, Fw 190 B and Fw 190 C – "which, with the exception of minor special equipment such as pressurised cabins or equipment for the use of GM 1 [nitrous oxide injection], were not specially designed for use in very great altitudes".

He said: "Before taking into account the measures available which can lead to an improvement in high-altitude performance, it must be stated in principle that the widely held view that increasing wing area offers a significant improvement in climb time and maximum ceiling is wrong".

The best ways of increasing climb time were, he said, increasing engine power or reducing weight. Work was already being undertaken based on a proposal by the RLM's C-E 2 department to improve the Bf 109's performance by eliminating all armour, saving 180kg. "Aircraft of this design are already running in series with the designation Bf 109 G-1/R2," he added.

Using GM 1 to improve performance had significant drawbacks though: "The addition of GM 1 is associated with a considerable weight expenditure due to the high consumption and the large container weights. GM 1 has great advantages for short-term increase in speed at high altitude, but due to the large additional weight only small benefits to improve climbing performance."

Engines were being designed specifically for use at high-altitude – the DB 614, DB 628 and BMW 8028 – but "only on a project basis". The engines would not be available in any numbers until 1944 at the earliest and when they were available the additional performance they offered had to be measured against their increased weight and drag. However, "of the mentioned high-altitude engines the installation of the DB 628 in the Bf 109 G should have the greatest prospects for the preparation of a good high-altitude fighter. Work to accelerate the provision of such engines, albeit in small numbers, should be made with utmost urgency. In cooperation between Messerschmitt and Daimler-Benz is currently an aircraft with DB 605 with intercooler (forerunner DB 628) being prepared. The experience gained here should serve for further work in this direction".

The DB 628 was essentially a DB 605 inverted V12, the powerplant intended to replace the 109's DB 601 for the G-series, but with two superchargers. Friebel said further improvements to the 109's altitude performance would be possible by reducing both the 109's fuel and ammunition load.

Generaloberst Hans Jeschonnek replied: "Reducing fuel, yes, reducing armament is a joke. If I have a high-altitude fighter and come close to the enemy and have no weapon to fight him, then that's useless."

The Inspekteur der Jagdflieger, Generalmajor Adolf Galland, added: "He will not get that far with the reduction of fuel."

ABOVE: The same BV 246 but this time the large hull of an unfinished BV 222 flying boat can also be seen in the background.

ABOVE: Blohm & Voss chief designer Richard Vogt, centre, pictured with aerodynamicist Ludwig Prandtl, left, and the director of the Deutschen Versuchsanstalt für Luftfahrt (DVL) Günter Bock, right.

ABOVE: Generalfeldmarschall Erhard Milch, head of the RLM, was a pivotal figure throughout the development of the Me 155 and BV 155.

Further discussion on this point followed before the Generalluftzeugmeister himself, Generalfeldmarschall Erhard Milch, said: "Then a question that is very important: whether one should develop with our normal gasoline engine a special high-altitude fighter, which is actually useful only at high altitude and with which one cannot fight in the intermediate altitudes."

Friebel responded: "The second question is whether it is time to divide the [current ongoing] development into a special high-altitude fighter, which can be designed properly for maximum altitude, but which, of course, is handicapped in intermediate altitudes by its larger wing surface area and all sorts of other things."

After some debate about the need for both day and night high-altitude fighters and whether evaporative cooling could be used to replace radiators to reduce drag, Luftwaffe staff officer Major Walter Storp said: "I think the Americans are working on the further development of the high-altitude aircraft. I do not know if they will make an appreciable appearance in 1942, but certainly in 1947 with bombers.

"For this reason, it seems necessary and expedient, apart from the interceptor thing and the special high-altitude, to try a special Bf 109 at least now. Because one thing seems to me a given: the demand for the highest altitude and the highest speed contradict each other – they are opposed. If I want to have greater speed, I inevitably come to a smaller wing area. For the high-altitudes I need a larger wing area.

"I would suggest that we prepare the Bf 109 developmentally in series with a larger area, to get safely to 13,000 to 14,000m."

Discussion then turned to the best engine for a special high-altitude fighter. RLM General-Ingenieur Wolfram Eisenlohr said: "The [DB] 605 was presented with a second turbine, which increases performance by 50%, so we would have 1200bhp instead of 750. Now the question is whether the aircraft conversion, which must be associated with it, comes to this mechanical solution at the same time. We can in the autumn have the first experimental aircraft. The 628 was the engine."

Milch said there were five more 'questions': what was the greatest altitude that could be achieved with a stripped-out but otherwise ordinary 109 carrying only a camera for reconnaissance; by a stripped-out 109 with normal weapons but only 50% of its usual ammunition; by a DB 628-powered but otherwise normal 109; by a 109 with DB 628 equipped for high-altitude flight, and by a 109 with DB 628 and enlarged wing surfaces.

The RLM's GL/C-B 3 (Engines) department director General-Ingenieur Franz Mahnke said Daimler-Benz was building only 150 DB 628s – due to be completed within a year. Milch said that for the time being this number did not need to be increased but asked about whether an exhaust gas turbine would be suitable for a high altitude fighter.

The head of development at the RLM, Gottfried Reidenbach, replied: "That question must be clarified in principle. The exhaust-gas turbine is a headache for the fighter pilot. When you apply the power, the exhaust-gas turbine does not start immediately. Whether this is at all acceptable for the single-seater, has to be tried first, one can not say that without further investigation."

Later on, progress on the 109's designated successor, the Me 309, was discussed. Work was under way on building the first 309 but there had been delays and the first example was not expected to be ready before October 1942. Milch stated that Messerschmitt had prepared a "purely experimental" backup in case the 309 was delayed still further – the Bf 109 H. This was to be a 109 "with stronger engine" but no further details were given.

No firm decisions appear to have arisen from the meeting but it was clear that the RLM already had several lines of development in progress which, it was hoped, would lead to a new fighter capable of meeting any high-altitude threat which the American air force might pose. It was also evident that Messerschmitt was heavily involved in this work while also being burdened with a multitude of simultaneous aircraft developments. It was a situation that would not improve as time wore on. ●

ABOVE LEFT: As Inspekteur der Jagdflieger in May 1942, Generalmajor Adolf Galland was involved in discussions about Messerschmitt's high-altitude fighters. He had little interest in the Me 155 or BV 155 but never actively opposed it. MIDDLE: Generaloberst Hans Jeschonnek argued against moves in 1942 to turn the Bf 109 into a high-altitude fighter simply by stripping it of armour and reducing both its fuel and weapons load. ABOVE RIGHT: Major Walter Storp, during a brief appointment to a staff position, voiced concerns that would dog the Luftwaffe throughout the war and keep the Me 155/BV 155 project alive even as others were being cancelled – that the Americans were developing high-altitude bombers which would be out of reach for all but the lowest-endurance German interceptors.

Chapter 2
Origins

May 1942 to April 1943
(Me 409, Me 155 and Me 209 Höhenjäger)

(12) DB 628

ABOVE: The Daimler-Benz DB 628 was a development of the DB 605 V12 fitted with a two-stage supercharger. Daimler-Benz began efforts to fit a DB 628 to a Messerschmitt Bf 109 airframe under the designation Me 409 in 1941. As work progressed, various changes to the airframe became necessary, including longer wings.

Messerschmitt's collaboration with Daimler-Benz to fit an early version of the DB 628 high-altitude engine to a Bf 109 had begun in 1941 under the internal company designation Me 409. This resulted in a longer-nosed aircraft with an extremely large spinner. Photographs from 1941, marked 'Me 409',[1] exist showing what appears to be a development mule DB 605/628 fitted to a Bf 109 airframe.

But while this work was still under way at Daimler-Benz in early 1942, Messerschmitt itself was struggling with the disastrous Me 210 programme, development of the Me 264 bomber, the Me 309 fighter, the Me 163 rocket fighter, the P 1065 jet fighter (soon to become the Me 262), the P 1079 pulsejet fighter (later the Me 328) and the Me 323 transport – while also supporting the ongoing development and production of the Bf 109 and Bf 110 fighters. None of it was going particularly smoothly.

A company memo dated March 20, 1942, headed 'Work for the French'[2] shows two projects being earmarked for subcontracting to unspecified aircraft companies in Vichy France. The first of these involved the design of a new wing for the Bf 109 G with improved landing flaps and larger ailerons; the second was an aircraft carrier version of the Bf 109 G with "catapult and tail hook equipment as 109 T".

It would also get new wings with a span increased from 9.925m to 11m and a wing area increased from 16.05m² to 19.4m². The carrier version would also have "undercarriage in wing (broad gauge)" – wide-set main wheels, better suited to deck landings than the original Bf 109's notoriously narrow undercarriage, which retracted inwards like those of the Fw 190.

Evidently Messerschmitt had received some advance warning of what was about to happen next. In early May, Adolf Hitler authorised the continuation of work on Germany's only aircraft carrier – the *Graf Zeppelin*. Although it had been launched in December 1938, work on the vessel had stopped in 1940 and the unfinished hull had been towed from harbour to harbour ever since to keep it out of harm's way.

According to a Messerschmitt document entitled Me 109 H Lebenslauf III/165/43, dated August 8, 1943 ('Lebenslauf' meaning 'curriculum vitae')[3], eight days after the GL-Besprechung where high-altitude fighters were discussed, on May 20, 1942, a meeting was held at Messerschmitt's Augsburg offices where the company received orders to develop a "Spezial-Träger-Jagdeinsitzer" and a "Spezial-Höhen-jäger" – a special single seat carrier fighter and a special high-altitude fighter. This double order was confirmed by letter on June 11.

The Lebenslauf document says: "Since the start-up of two special aircraft in development and production was practically hopeless, an Me 109 G with an enlarged wing area and a stronger chassis was selected, especially with regard to a rapid manufacturing process for the carrier aircraft. At the same time, two wing root MG 151s were provided to reinforce the armament.

"For the purpose of secondary use, by replacing the DB 605 with the DB 628 and by adding enlarged edge caps, it could become an altitude fighter able to meet the requirements of the time (maximum altitude 14km). This model, which was given the designation Me 155, was first developed very slowly in Paris."

While it may be succinct, this summary is somewhat over-simplified. Messerschmitt had nominally begun development of a 109 G-based carrier aircraft in France two months before it received the order to do so. And when the high-altitude development was tacked on, this too was handed to the company's subcontractor Société nationale des constructions aéronautiques du Nord, aka SNCAN, at Les Mureaux on the western outskirts of Paris.

The French were told that what they were working on was the Me 409. This fact would later be mentioned to Allied intelligence officers Major John W Logan of the US Army Air Corps and Arthur Woodward Nutt of the British Ministry of Aircraft Production when, in the aftermath of the liberation of Paris, they were compiling a report[4] on work carried by French companies for the Germans in the city.

On June 25, less than a fortnight after the double 'special aircraft' order was confirmed, a meeting was held in Berlin between Messerschmitt and RLM representatives to discuss the Me 409's undercarriage[5]. This states that "the type Me 409 is provided with DB 605 for carrier use, with Jumo 213 for normal fighter use and with DB 628 as high-altitude fighter. The starting weights are, according to Messerschmitt AG, 3.5 tons as carrier aircraft, 4.1 tons as normal fighter and 3.75 tons as high-altitude fighter. The other dimensions are wing area 19.5m² and span 11m in normal fighter and carrier aircraft, and for high-altitude fighter wing area is 21m² and span 12.85m".

Meanwhile, separate development work slowly continued on plans to fit a DB 628 to an ordinary Bf 109 – without the Me 409's wing and undercarriage alterations – as the stripped out but otherwise production standard high-altitude fighter outlined by Friebel during the GL-Besprechung on May 12.

Abschrift

Der Reichsminister der Luftfahrt   Adlershof, den 25.6.1942
St/GL/C-E 2/Festigkeitsprüfstelle
    Nr. 313 / 42 geh.   *Me 155*

                                           1.Ausfertigung

Vorläufige Festigkeitsvorschriften Me 409 Fahrwerk.

Besprechung am 25.6.42 in Adlershof.
Anwesend : Ostertag Mtt.AG Otto Schulz} C-e 2 / FP

Ferngespräch Elbelt (E-Stelle Travemünde) - Otto (C-E 2 / FP) am
24.6.42.

Das Muster Me 409 wird mit DB 605 für Trägereinsatz,mit Jumo 213
für normalen Jagdeinsatz und mit DB 628 als Höhenjäger vorgesehen.
Die Startgewichte sind nach Angabe von Mtt.AG. G= 3,5 to als
Trägerflugzeug, G= 4,1 to als normaler Jäger und G= 3,75 to als
Höhenjäger. Die weiteren Abmessungen sind F= 19,5 m², und
b = 11 m bei normaler Jäger und beim Trägerflugzeug; beim Höhenjäger ist F = 21 m² und b = 12,85 m.

1. Die sichere Stossgeschwindigkeit für Hauptfahrwerk und Sporn
   wird für das Startgewicht beim normalen Jäger aus der Bezie-
   hung
$$v_{st} = 1,5 + 0,2 \sqrt{G/F} \text{ ermittelt.}$$
   Damit ergibt sich für das Gewicht G = 4,1 to die Stossgeschwindigkeit zu v_{st} = 4,4 m/s. Für das Startgewicht von G = 3,5 to
   entsprechend dem Trägereinsatz ergibt sich dann eine aufnehm-
   bare sichere Stoßgeschwindigkeit von v_{st} 4,75 m/s. Diese Stoßgeschwindigkeit wird als ausreichend angesehen. Eine Abfanghöhe
   von 3 m dürfte damit noch gedeckt sein.

2. Die Fallhöhe für den Fall 230 (Fallstoss) ist für das normale
   Startgewicht zu ermitteln aus
$$h = 1,7 \frac{(1+0,03 \, v_L)^2}{2g} - f_1$$
   und für das Überlaststartgewicht aus
$$h = \frac{(1+0,03 \, v_L)^2}{2g}$$

3. Der Fall 250 (Kurvenrollen) ist für das grösste Überlaststartgewicht mit n_y = 0,5 nachzuweisen.

4. Für den Fall 222 werden zur Berücksichtigung der Beanspruchun-
   gen bei Seitenwindlandungen mit Querneigung die gleichen Stoß-
   kräfte angesetzt wie im Fall 221. Die Seitenkräfte werden in
   den Fällen 221 und 222 zu P_y = 0,3 P_z angenommen. Ausser der
   normalen Stosskraftrichtung in den Fällen 221 und 222 ist auch
   eine um 20° geneigte Stosskraftrichtung anzusetzen.

5. Für den Katapultstart wird eine Beschleunigung von 4,5 g angenommen.

6. Die am Landehaken angreifenden Kräfte werden entspr. einer Ver-
   zögerung von 4 g angesetzt.

                                                         -2-

Only July 22, the RLM's C-E 2 department produced a document entitled 'Strength requirements for V-pattern Me 155'[6] which referenced the June meeting on the Me 409 but also said: "The pattern Me 109 H is to be used as a single seat fighter for carrier and land use, as well as high-altitude fighter." It repeated exactly the same data given at the June meeting concerning the weight, wing area and wingspan of the normal, carrier and high-altitude versions of the type before outlining the necessary structural load for each version. Given that the technical details supplied for the Me 409 on June 25 were identical to those given for the Bf 109 H on July 22, 1942, it would appear that they were one and the same thing at this point.

But now neither type number applied, because the normal/carrier/high-altitude fighter project had been awarded the new RLM designation Me 155 (8-155). The 'Me 409' name disappeared for good, but 'Bf 109 H' would re-emerge later.

The RLM's Entwicklungsbesprechung or 'development meeting' on October 9, 1942[7], received a brief update on progress with the DB 628 and was told that "since the engine is slightly longer in total, there is an influence on the centre of gravity. [But] the installation does not present any special problems (compared to the difficult exhaust pipes of the TK 9). DB 628 is intended for Bf 109 G.

From October 27 to November 2, 1942, engineer Fach from the Luftwaffe's E-Stelle Tarnewitz went on a business trip to Messerschmitt's headquarters at Augsburg and reported back on the company's latest developments – including the Me 323, Me 163 B, Me 210/410, Me 328, Me 329, Me 309, Bf 110 with Flak 18 and finally the high-altitude version of the

ABOVE: The Graf Zeppelin aircraft carrier shortly after its launch in 1938. Work on completing it was halted in 1940 before recommencing in 1942. The fighter originally designed for it, the Bf 109 T, was now outdated – prompting a requirement for a revised and updated carrier fighter.

OPPOSITE: A page from an RLM report dated June 25, 1942, showing that the Me 409 project had been split into three strands – a carrier aircraft powered by a DB 605, a Jumo 213-powered 'normal' fighter and a high-altitude fighter with a DB 628. The first two would have an 11m wingspan while the latter would have a span of 12.85m. Soon after the Me 409 received the formal RLM designation Me 155.

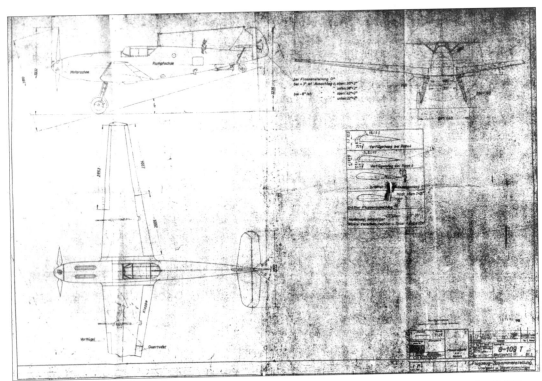

ABOVE: Factory drawing of the Messerschmitt Bf 109 T carrier fighter from 1940. The 'T' was based on the Bf 109 E-7 but fitted with new 11m span wings. Wings of that span would have been used for the Me 409/Me 155 carrier and 'normal' fighters – the key difference being a wide track undercarriage where the Bf 109 T retained the standard 109's narrow track.

Me 155. In his report of November 3, 1942[8], he wrote: "Me 155 is development of the Bf 109 G with DB 628. Enlargement of the wings by means of intermediate piece between the fuselage and the normal wings. Armament: motor cannon MG 151/20 or MK 108. The fuselage armament must be omitted because of lack of space (DB 628).

The design of the Me 155 had evidently received an update to keep it in line with the overall development of the 109 components it was expected to share. A company data sheet of November 13, 1942[9] discussed the aircraft's carrier form and reported on the "condition of the aircraft – airframe as the Me 109 G-1 with the following changes taken into account: enlarged wing area, attachment of catapult fittings and hooks. Remarks: On the airframe side, the following changes have been made compared to the data sheets IV/25/42 and IV/26/42 – gondola weapons are deleted, tailwheel completely retractable. Radiator and propeller: according to G-1 version". The old 409/109 H underpinnings were gone and the Me 155 was now a full member of the Bf 109 G family.

The aircraft's engine was the DB 605 A, wingspan was 14.06m, wing area was 19.4m² and length was 8.95m. Armament was two MG 131s on the nose with 250 rounds each, an MG 151 with 220 rounds firing through the spinner and two more MG 151s in the wings with 240 rounds each.

It must be concluded that between May and November 1942, the Me 409/Bf 109 H/ Me 155 existed as little more than a handful of drawings and calculations. The high-altitude fighter version in particular was put very much on the back burner while what little development effort there was to spare was concentrated on the aircraft carrier version.

The Me 109 H Lebenslauf says that the reason for the Me 155's lack of progress "was the start-up of the new SNCAN construction offices, and the lack of support from the local representative of the Augsburg project office; it was fully utilised by the Me 309 development work".

ME 155 VERSUS ME 309

The tricycle undercarriage Me 309 was the designated successor to the Bf 109 series. It is unsurprising that Messerschmitt's Paris office had utilised the resources at its disposal for work on the Me 309 since the troubled type had consistently lagged behind schedule and had been given emergency development priority by the RLM during an Entwicklungsbesprechung on September 11, 1942[10].

On November 24, 1942, Messerschmitt produced a report detailing how the Me 155 and Me 309 could each be made to carry a 1000kg SC1000 bomb[11]. This appears to have been a thinly veiled attempt to offer the RLM a cheap Schnellstbomber or 'fast bomber' which would negate the need for the competition of that name which was nearing its conclusion by this time. The report says: "Maximum speed with bomb attached or with bomb container is in both cases nearly 450km/h and over 500km/h respectively so barely behind the specially developed designs. After dropping the bomb load, on the other hand, speed increases by 80-170km/h depending on the pattern."

Creating the fast bomber Me 155 from the normal machine required a few changes however. The DB 605-powered Me 155 would need all its weapons and accessories removed

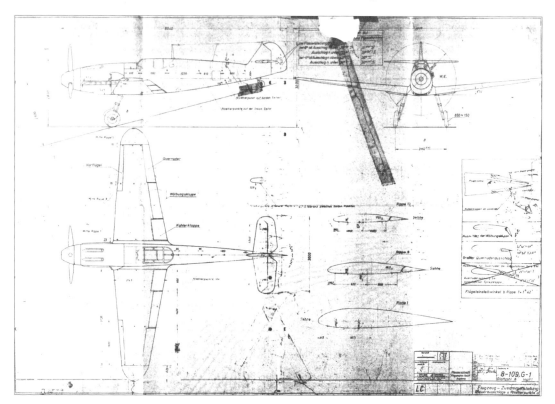

ABOVE: Drawing of the Bf 109 G-1 dated July 25, 1941. The Me 409/Me 155 was largely based on early G-series components.

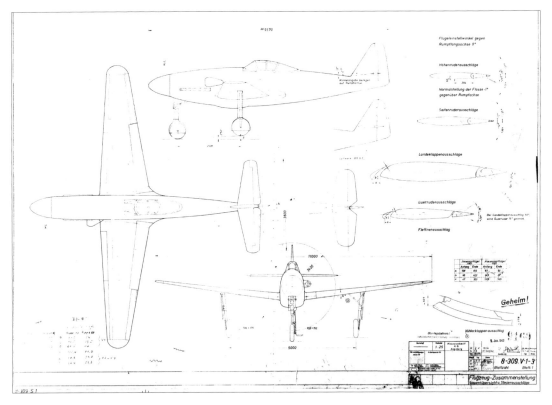

ABOVE: A significant part of the development work for the Bf 109's successor, the Me 309, was carried out by Messerschmitt's French subcontractors – taking vital capacity away from the Me 155. This drawing, dated May 29, 1942, shows some of the different tail fins and tailplanes considered for the troubled aircraft.

– except for the MG 151 motor cannon. An additional 200 litre fuel tank would be installed in the fuselage and the retractable tailwheel would be replaced with a fixed one from the Me 110 B, giving ground clearance of 50mm.

It is unclear whether this design was ever submitted for the Schnellstbomber competition – which was won on January 19, 1943, by the Dornier P 231[12], soon to be given the designation Do 335.

The Me 155's potential new fast bomber role was hardly mentioned during a meeting in Paris on November 26, 1942, between E-Stelle Travemünde representative Königs and Messerschmitt's area manager Fritz Hügelschäffer. The minutes[13], which refer to the 'Me 155' throughout, are further evidence that by this time the normal fighter and high-altitude fighter versions of the aircraft were simply not being worked on. In fact, throughout this period no known document ever refers to an 'Me 155 A', 'Me 155 B' or 'Me 155 C' (or, indeed, a 'Bf 109 ST') – there was only the Me 155 and this name is nearly always used to refer to the carrier version of the design. Mentions of a high-altitude Messerschmitt design are generally reserved for the separate Bf 109 G with DB 628 development.

The first point on the agenda for the meeting was the potential replacement of the Me 155's MG 151 motor cannon with the MK 108, which was due to be installed in production model Bf 109 Gs. The second point concerned the undercarriage and the need for bigger main wheels if larger loads were to be carried.

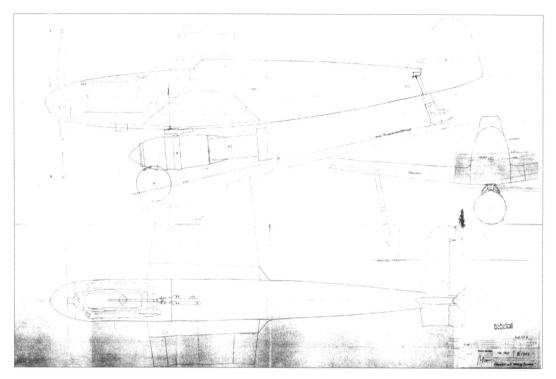

ABOVE: During discussions about creating a new lightweight Schnellbomber for the Luftwaffe in November 1942, Messerschmitt produced 'Schnellbomber' designs for both the Me 155 and Me 309. For the Me 155, further modifications to the Me 109 G-1 derived airframe would include a long fixed tailwheel, removal of all armour and armament reduced to just an MG 151 motor cannon.

The launch of the Me 155 using a catapult, with acceleration of 1.5g, was possible up to an all-up weight of 3.8 tons and "contrary to Messerschmitt AG's guidelines for the construction of carrier aircraft (maximum span 11m), the span of the Me 155 can be increased in case of need up to a maximum of 12m. (According to the E-Stelle Travemünde the lift width is 14m)".

A trial landing arrestor hook had been designed by Messerschmitt in Augsburg based on a proposal supplied by Travemünde and plans were being prepared for installing it. A number of Bf 109 Ts were to be supplied to Augsburg by Travemünde the following month – although the exact purpose of this transfer of old 109 Ts is unclear. Finally, "in order to eliminate difficulties in material procurement and labour issues, the E-Stelle Travemünde is trying to reach the emergency level priority for Me 155".

Another E-Stelle Tarnewitz engineer, Karsten, met with Messerschmitt representatives during a trip to the RLM in Berlin from December 1-3, 1942, to discuss the Me 155's armament. His report of December 5[14] states: "Fuselage and equipment should largely be taken over by Bf 109 G. Provided with wide landing gear, it should be used as a carrier aircraft. The armament consists of: 1 MG 151/20 firing in the engine with 220 rounds, 2 MG 151/20 firing in the wing roots with 240 rounds each, 2 MG 131 firing in the wings with 250 rounds each."

The frantic scramble to develop the Me 155's carrier form continued into 1943. According to a summary of the Entwicklungsbesprechung held on January 8, 1943[15], the head of the ministry's C-B department Heinrich Hertel said that "the aircraft carrier *Graf Zeppelin* is to be put into service on October 1, 1943. Beginning of the full aviation training on board March 15, 1944. The following dates are for the Me 155: V1 cleared for flight testing July 15, 1943. V2 September and V3 November. Further prototypes January to July 1944. Series production from February 1, 1944. First production aircraft August 15, 1944 further planning on 15 aircraft per month. Already these dates can be kept only with special measures (material delivery, transfer of the French constructors to Germany, provision of the work for the series)".

At the same meeting, the parallel development of the standard Bf 109 with DB 628 was also discussed. It was reported by Friebel that "a special gain in speed compared to DB 605 is expected from the propeller development. However, there are difficulties in making it possible to accommodate larger propeller diameters due to the lack of ground clearance of the Bf 109". Oberstabsingenieur Mann reported that the DB 628 was on schedule – with the first examples expected to become available for flight testing at the end of the month. By April 25, 1943, it was expected that a total of 150 engines would have been constructed with another 300 by April 1, 1944.

The chief of the RLM's technical office Oberstleutnant Wolfgang Vorwald told the meeting that "Of the fifty Bf 109 G-3s with pressurised cabins due to be available in February 1943, 25 are planned for DB 605 with GM 1 and 25 for DB 628". Milch apparently agreed that the DB 628 was of particular importance due to the continuous performance that a two-stage turbo offered over a single stage with GM 1. He closed by saying that "at the same time the task is to bring the fighter to an altitude of 16km".

CANCELLED!

At the beginning of 1943 it was clear that the type responsible for starving the Me 155 of design and development capacity, the Me 309, was going badly wrong. The nosewheel tended to block airflow to the radiator positioned directly behind it on take-off and in the air it offered little in the way of a performance improvement over the Bf 109 G. Directional stability issues had resulted in plans for a much larger tailfin and perhaps most damningly of all, it had been determined that it would be difficult to mass produce.

On January 15 Messerschmitt produced a document entitled Comparison Me 209 – 309[16], which offered "preliminary remarks about the performance sheets". Under "condition of the aircraft" the document states that the Me 209 comprised "109 G fuselage with unit engine DB 603, 109 G wing with intermediate piece for surface enlargement, by eliminating the wing radiator flaps according to Me 309".

Remarkably, although it was essentially just another member of the extensive 109 G family, the Me 209 of January 1943 appears to have resulted from a revival of the old Me 209 development work dating back to 1937. In its original form, the 209 was a small monoplane aircraft designed to break the world air speed record – which it did on April 26, 1939, at 756km/h (469mph). Efforts to develop the 209 into a fighter continued into 1940 and aerodynamics work on the fuselage and wings continued into August 1941, with the design becoming progressively larger and the cockpit being moved from the rear of the fuselage to the centre.

After a gap of about 12 months, aerodynamics work resumed in August 1942 but it would appear that Messerschmitt eventually reached the conclusion that there was little to be gained by retaining anything of the aircraft's original fuselage and therefore opted to simply replace it with the 109 G assembly. A wide-track undercarriage was included as part of the wing extension. In a roundabout way, therefore, it came to resemble the Me 155.

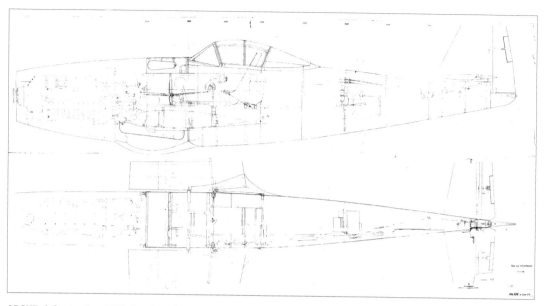

ABOVE: A September 1942 drawing of the Me 309 fitted with a Jumo 213 engine. Fitment of the 213 was planned as early as 1941 but projections for its availability proved to be somewhat optimistic.

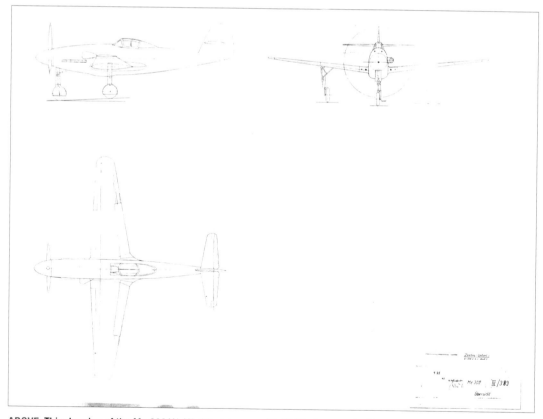

ABOVE: This drawing of the Me 309 V1-V3 dated January 15, 1943, shows a significantly enlarged tailfin. Just six days later, a meeting of the RLM's Entwicklungsbesprechung would hear that the Me 309 was not suitable for mass production "in its planned form".

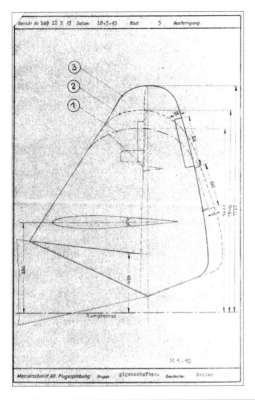

At an Entwicklungsbesprechung on January 21, 1943[17], it was announced that, following a discussion the previous day between Willy Messerschmitt, Galland and Vorwald, the official replacement for the Bf 109 was to become the Me 209. A summary of the meeting states: "The total capacity for Me 309 is reallocated for this purpose. The development of the Me 309 will be discontinued with the proviso that it may be resumed at a later date in conjunction with a more powerful engine such as DB 609."

Vorwald reported: "The main features of the Me 209 compared to Bf 109 are: DB 603 G, Fw 190 undercarriage, so wide wheel track, much stronger armament (1 x MK 103, 2 x MK 108, 2 x MG 151, 2 x MG 131). The flight performance is equal to the Me 309, the climb performance even better. Since development and production can rely to a

LEFT: Three different potential tail forms for the Bf 109 H from the May 18, 1943, report.

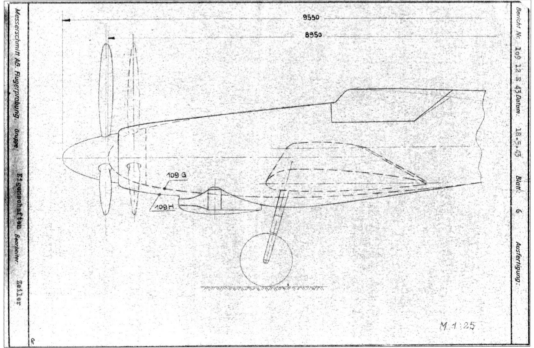

ABOVE: With development work on the Me 155 halted on February 23, 1943, the Bf 109 H became Messerschmitt's sole ongoing high-altitude fighter project. This drawing, from a report dated May 18, 1943, shows how the installation of the DB 628 would change the aircraft's forward profile compared to the standard Bf 109 G.

considerable extent on components and equipment of Bf 109, the effort [required to bring it to full production] according to Messerschmitt is only 25% compared to Me 309. As a result, a significant production gain can be achieved going forward. Moreover, Messerschmitt, after a thorough examination, reported that task Me 309 was not suitable for mass production in the planned form."

Messerschmitt had give a set of sketchy dates for development of the Me 209: prototypes towards the end of 1943, pre-production full scale testing at the beginning of 1944 and the prospect of a twin fuselage variant had also been discussed since "the question Me 209 Zwilling is reserved for a later decision".

The cancellation of the Me 309 was followed not long after by the cancellation of the Me 155. At the end of January it was ordered that all work on the *Graf Zeppelin* aircraft carrier should cease. This effectively made the Me 155 redundant, although the order took nearly three weeks to come through. Willy Messerschmitt himself sent a letter to the company's Berlin office on February 19, 1943[18], saying that "the Me 155 series is stopped and immediately shut down. Subcontractors must be notified accordingly. I ask you to arrange that urgently the development of the 155 is shut down. There is no sense continuing if no series comes".

Messerschmitt AG managing director Rakan Kokothaki wrote to the Messerschmitt offices in Paris the following day[19] regarding "taking care of the construction bureaus of SNCAN and Avions Caudron". He wrote: "I read your message and I must emphasise that the experience of designing parts of the Me 155 in Paris shows that the handling of such things in France is not responsible. So many good engineers must be sent to France that it is even better to bring fewer Frenchmen here."

He said he had sent some of the company's best engineers to Paris but results had not been forthcoming. Perhaps some work could be carried out in Paris under close supervision, he said, but it was better to keep designers at Augsburg. He added: "It may be that Paris also has well-managed design offices, but unfortunately we have not had the good fortune to come to such cooperation."

ME 209 HÖHENJÄGER

The loss of the Me 309 and Me 155 cleared the decks somewhat at Messerschmitt. Having had so much of its project work fall by the wayside, the company grasped the opportunities offered by the Me 209 with both hands. Three days after Kokothaki's letter to Messerschmitt's Paris office, on February 22, 1943, representatives of Messerschmitt met with staff from the RLM's C-E 2 department in Berlin to discuss requirements for the Me 209 programme.

The RLM's report on the meeting, issued on March 5[20], stated that the Me 209 "should be used primarily as a normal fighter aircraft. It is equipped with five weapons (1 x MK 108, 2 x MG 131 in the fuselage, 2 x MG 151 in the wing roots). It should also be used with 9 weapons as a heavy fighter or as a ground-attack aircraft (in addition 4 x MK 108 in the structure). In addition, use as fighter-bomber (3 weapons and 1000kg bomb), long-range fighter bomber (3 weapons, 500kg bomb and 2 x 300 litre additional fuel tanks) as well as reconnaissance and high-altitude fighter is provided.

"Messerschmitt is currently giving the following data: take-off weight as fighter 4 tons, maximum take-off weight as fighter-bomber 4.88 tons. Take-off weight as attack aircraft 4.74 tons (including 275kg additional armour). Wing area 16.4m², wingspan 10m. For use as high-altitude fighter and as attack aircraft an enlarged wing area with 21.6m² is provided.

Wingspan is 13m. Engine is DB 603. In addition, eventual possibility to install BMW 801, Jumo 213 and Jumo 222. Greatest horizontal speed with DB 603 570km/h at ground level and 725km/h at 7km altitude".

The company eventually got around to issuing a full technical description of the Me 209 Höhenjäger on April 13, 1943[21], based on drawing number III/447.

This indicated that in order to shift the centre of gravity to compensate for the length of the DB 628 engine, the aircraft's wings were to be shifted rearwards by 260mm compared to those of the standard Me 209. And the 13m wingspan mentioned during the February 22 meeting was to be achieved by inserting a rectangular wing centrepiece which would contain the radiators. There were two options for how these would be arranged – either the same system as the Bf 109 G with underwing radiators and expansion flaps or with radiators "similar to the de Havilland Mosquito in wing leading edge". Wing area was down slightly to 21.5m².

If the Bf 109 G radiator setup was adopted an additional 100 litre fuel tank could be installed in each wing ahead of the spar. The Mosquito-style option was "dependant on an aerodynamic investigation which has not yet been completed".

The standard Me 209 fuselage was to be used but with a number of amendments mostly necessitated by the shifted wing position: expanded ammunition storage, new engine and wing connection fittings, changes to the fuselage sides, change of controls and flap operations, change of panels under the fuselage to accommodate the DB 628, alterations to the fuel tank compartment and possible alterations to the fuel line routing.

Neither the aircraft's tail nor its undercarriage differed from those of the standard fighter model. The engine was to be installed in the same way as it was in the Me 109 G but with propeller diameter increased from 3m to 3.4m and with the upper cowling modified.

The Me 209 Höhenjäger was unarmoured with the exception of the windscreen and armament consisted of either an MK 108 or MG 151 motor cannon plus two MG 151s which were positioned one metre out from the wing roots. There wasn't room to fit an MK 103 or the Me 209's standard bomb rack fittings. Maximum take-off weight was 3850kg – slightly lighter than the standard fighter despite its larger wings. Finally, the description states "performances correspond to those of the high-altitude fighter Me 155. For details see enclosed data sheets."

The Me 109 H Lebenslauf document neatly sums up this stage of Messerschmitt's convoluted high-altitude fighter development programme: "After the carrier programme had been stopped in January 1943, and the Me 155 carrier aircraft had been stopped, the high-altitude fighter version was changed from the basis of the Me 155 to the basis of the Me 209, which had replaced the Me 309. The offer of a 'Me 209 Höhenjäger with DB 628' was submitted to the RLM's Technical Office on April 23, 1943. The performance offered by this project was practically the same as that of the Me 155 high-altitude fighter version."

In parallel to the abrupt revival of the Me 209 name and the positioning of this new Bf 109 G series derivative as the chosen successor to the Bf 109 itself, work steadily continued on efforts to fit the DB 628 to an otherwise standard Bf 109. The Bf 109 H name was now applied to this project. Where the first 'H' had used the letter only because it was next in line after the preceding G-series, this new 'H' stood for 'Höhenjäger'.

However, neither the Me 209 Höhenjäger nor the Bf 109 H was a bespoke high-altitude fighter – both hedged their bets by offering a decent maximum service ceiling while

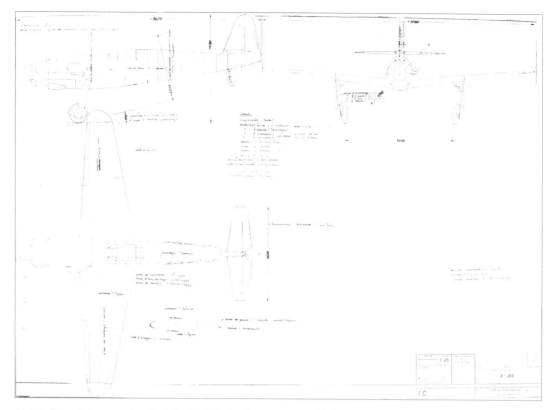

ABOVE: When it became clear that the Me 309 development was unlikely to reach series production, Messerschmitt went back to the drawing board and came up with a new version of the Me 209 – in reality another heavily modified Bf 109 G. This drawing with French annotations dates from early 1943.

retaining a measure of combat performance at lower altitudes. But the RLM was growing increasingly concerned that this would not be enough if the Americans managed to bring a machine into service that could fly above 14,000m. What they really wanted was an 'Extremen Höhenjäger'. ●

Chapter 3
Blohm & Voss to the rescue
May 1943 to September 1943
(P 1091 and Me 155 B)

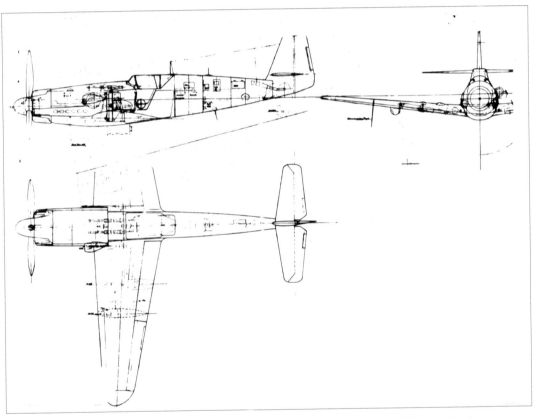

ABOVE: This sketchy and undated drawing of the Me 209 appears to date from summer 1943, given the heavy armament it is shown carrying. This design formed the basis for the Me 209 H.

The Me 209 Höhenjäger was presented to the RLM on April 23, 1943, and 11 days later, on May 4, ministry staff engineer Schwarz arrived at Messerschmitt's Augsburg offices for a meeting to discuss it[1]. According to a company memo dated the following day, Schwarz asked for performance data on the standard Me 209 when fitted with a DB 603 engine and boosted by GM 1 injection for 20 minutes. He also wanted directly comparable data on the flight duration of the Me 209 Höhenjäger "which was offered to the Technical Office as a replacement for the Me 155".

Schwarz then explained that "there is interest in a fighter with an extreme maximum altitude. Load assumptions in this case are still unknown". He offered the Messerschmitt team some rather vague guidelines for their "preliminary investigations" including armament of one MK 108 and two MG 151s – which was what the Me 209 Höhenjäger already had. Minimum ceiling was 12km and fuel capacity needed to be at least 400 litres. Four different engines were to be considered: DB 628, DB 627, DB 603 with Hirth exhaust-driven turbosupercharger and DB 603 with GM 1 injection. The aircraft's primary role was as a fighter but it also had to be useable for reconnaissance.

Schwarz said he would give Messerschmitt two weeks to get started then make a return visit and "until then, the preliminary examinations should be as open to discussion as possible". He also told the Messerschmitt team that Focke-Wulf had built a high-altitude fighter wing in France which had a surface area 2m² greater than that of the standard Fw 190. Efforts were being made, he said, to fit an Fw 190 with a DB 603 engine which incorporated a Hirth turbosupercharger but "the exhaust and charge air ducts are routed outboard of the fuselage and cause considerable drag".

By May 11, Messerschmitt had begun a new project designated P 1091 to see what creating a new extreme high-altitude fighter would entail. The man in charge was Fritz Hügelschäffer, who had previously overseen the Me 155. He wrote a memo that day headed 'High-altitude aircraft P 1091; radiator dimensions'[2], which stated: "For the P 1091 aircraft we need radiator weights and drag. Above all, we need a graph showing radiator weight over radiator drag resistance. The radiator should have as little aerodynamic drag as possible in the climb."

It was already clear to Hügelschäffer that designing effective radiators for an aircraft flying at extremely high-altitude was going to be difficult. Large and very heavy radiators would be needed and the level of drag they produced was likely to make or break the aircraft as an effective fighter.

For the purposes of this calculation, the P 1091 was to be considered as fitted with the DB 628 and the coolant heat that would need to be dispersed at 11km altitude was 360,000kcal per hour, in addition to 48,500kcal from the lubricant. Exhaust gases would also need cooling from 180° to 100° before they could enter the turbocharger. The air circulation routing was to be taken over from the DB 628-powered Bf 109 H as far as possible because engine testing with that type was about to commence.

Hügelschäffer wrote a very similar memo the following day[3] asking for graphs relating to radiators required by the DB 603 A when paired with the Hirth TK 11 turbocharger. The Messerschmitt Probü or 'projects office' wrote a memo to Hügelschäffer on May 18, 1943, headed 'Höhenjäger with DB 627'[4] which said: "On the basis of more recent installation investigations, it has been found that the DB 627 in the Me 209 is fairly cheap to install. The use of the unit drum radiator is not practical for centre of gravity reasons. However, the entire cooling system for charge air as well as for lubricant and main water circuit can be accommodated in the centre section of the high-altitude fighter's wing between the fuselage and the outer wing. The installation of the MG 131 has not been investigated, but it is unlikely to be carried out. MK 108 or 103 installation is possible."

On May 25 the Probü was investigating the efficiency of a 3.7m diameter propeller for the DB 628 with the aim of maintaining a good rate of climb at 2km, 6km and 9km altitudes[5]. And on June 11, 1943, Hirth informed Messerschmitt that its new TKL 15 turbosupercharger for the DB 603 was expected to be ready by the end[6] of the year and that "the performance data shown in the engine brochure are achieved with certainty and the actual performance is expected to be slightly higher".

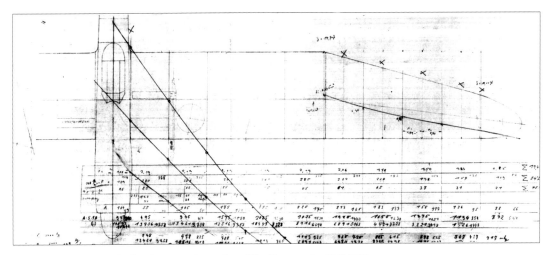

ABOVE: Mid-1943 sketch showing an early version of the Messerschmitt P 1091.

That same day Vorwald told an Entwicklungsbesprechung[7] that Daimler-Benz had been given a deadline of June 17 to complete the first fully operational DB 628 engine installation in a Bf 109. A flight test three weeks after that "must give a clear picture of the suitability of the DB 628". It had been apparent for some time that the DB 628, upon which so many hopes had been pinned since 1941, was not living up to expectations. Four days later, on June 15, 1943, a further Entwicklungsbesprechung was held at which Milch ordered Daimler-Benz to attend a meeting with him on June 18 to discuss the future of the DB 628 and ongoing issues with the DB 605[8].

What was said during the meeting is unclear but later that day RLM engineer Schwarz rang the Messerschmitt Probü to announce that a meeting on high-altitude fighters was to be held on June 23 at the RLM's offices in Berlin[9]. He also enquired about the performance of the normal Me 209 when fitted with a TKL 15-boosted DB 603. The substance of that meeting may be inferred by an order issued the following day, June 24, by Probü chief Woldemar Voigt[10]. He asked that drawings of the "extremen höhenjäger mit TK 15" along with whatever performance data on it was available should be sent to Messerschmitt's Berlin office as a matter of urgency "as these documents will probably be required tomorrow for the Secretary of State [Milch]".

The next day, June 25, the first item on the Entwicklungsbesprechung's agenda was fighters[11]. According to a summary of the minutes, Milch ordered that "in one of the next development discussions, it should be presented which measures, with the least expenditure on design and capacity, are necessary to bring engines of the 2000-2200hp class into production for fighters as soon as practicably possible".

He ordered Willy Messerschmitt and Focke-Wulf chief designer Kurt Tank to submit performance data, with special consideration given to high-altitude performance, weights and operational possibilities for their next generation fighters. And "since the Me 209, even if it could be built at Messerschmitt, would not enter series production before summer 1945 and as far as the high-altitude variant is concerned it is to be considered whether it would be an earlier and more tangible solution to use the Bf 109 continuation or Fw 190 as the basis instead".

Vorwald told the meeting that "according to Daimler-Benz the DB 603 with 2500hp is expected within one and a half to two years. For this comparatively small engine an aircraft in the order of Me 209 would be suitable. This is still under investigation by C-E and Messerschmitt. For weight comparison with the Fw 190, however, it should be noted that the Me 209 is not yet designed in high-altitude form and the weight of the finished aircraft is usually greater than the value previously stated in the draft proposal".

MANPOWER SHORTAGE

On June 26, 1943, the Probü produced a short report entitled simply 'P 1091 Höhenjäger mit TK 15'[12] which detailed an aircraft with a 21m wingspan, 39m² wing area, pressure cabin and DB 603 A engine with Hirth TK 15 turbosupercharger. It would be armed with an MK 108 motor cannon and two MG 151s or two further MK 108s in the wings. Carrying up to 1000kg of bombs would also be possible. The appended drawing, number III/474, showed a very long-winged aircraft with a slightly bulbous fuselage and a contra-rotating double propeller. The report was signed by both Voigt and Hügelschäffer and two copies were sent to Schwarz at the RLM.

During a discussion about the Me 262 at a GL-Besprechung on June 29[13], Milch told Willy Messerschmitt: "For you, Messerschmitt, it would be much happier if at any time you could pass from the 109 perfectly to the 262, at first in the normal version and later the high-altitude variation of it. Then you would not have to bring your whole apparatus again to the 209. That would be good for us."

Messerschmitt replied that it didn't matter which aircraft you modified for high-altitude work, the result would be the same: "One would have to rebuild each aircraft considerably. With the normal wing surface area, it is not possible. You have to increase the area. We get the most out of the engine by increasing the wingspan. With the 109, for example, by adding intermediate sections you can increase the span. This is a comparatively simple conversion."

Later on, Milch asked directly: "When would series production start, if the 209 was the basis for the high altitude type?" Messerschmitt replied: "I have not thought about that yet."

Milch then said: "A comparison with the 190 would be necessary. We also have to discuss with Focke-Wulf this question – which variant comes faster and which promises more success. I do not think you want to burden yourself with a 209 high-altitude variant, if it is not necessary.

Messerschmitt said: "If it is not necessary, then no. I only fear that it will be necessary. I think something needs to be done. Otherwise, the English will one day come in with high-flying aircraft to Berlin."

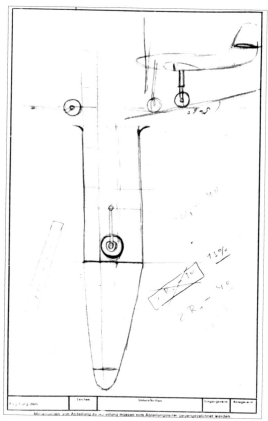

ABOVE: This undated Messerschmitt sketch from a file of papers on the P 1091 seems to suggest that a tricycle undercarriage configuration was considered for the design at one point.

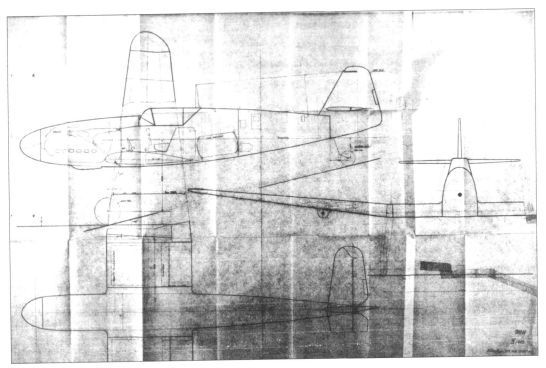

ABOVE: Messerschmitt drawing III/483 showing the '109 H – Höhenjäger 109 with DB 605 + O2'. The same drawing would later be repurposed to represent the P 1091 Stage 1.

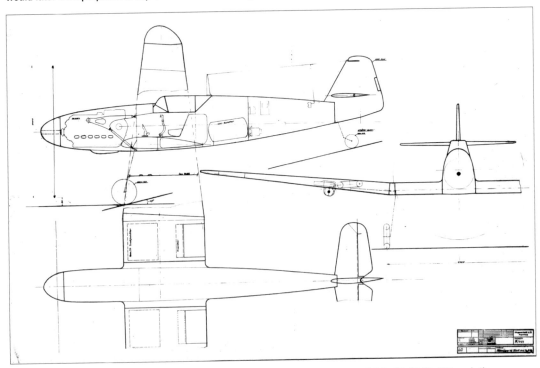

ABOVE: A second version of the III/483 drawing from the P 1091 project report of July 26, 1943. Although the description remains the same, '109 H' is missing.

The discussion then turned to the Me 262 and Messerschmitt production director Fritz Hentzen, who was present with Messerschmitt himself and Kokothaki, said that the company required another 125 men for the development programme. Having evidently heard this sort of request from Messerschmitt too many times previously, Milch replied angrily: "What would you have done if the 209 had to start? Let me tell you something – I have strained over your requests because you are doing something new. But in all seriousness, it's not like we had the resources in our pockets, on the left side, on the right side, or stuck down behind the machine tools, so that we only ever had to pick them out and say: here they are. You know that's not the case.

"This is a busy industry. Of course, you always have to try to bring in extra resources, and nobody will deny that we did that. We [the air ministry] also do not have the people ourselves, we have to take them from others. We do not get any staff for two months, but we have departures due to fluctuation, expiration of contracts, confiscation to the Wehrmacht, etc. We must honestly try to help ourselves.

"Despite rationalisation, we keep trying to come up with the goods, we try to pump in what we can get, designers etc. The total capacity in the field, Messerschmitt, is much too small. One and a half years ago – we know what we discussed back then – it was about 28 designers, then about 80, then it was again a new sum. We will try again. But you also have to help yourself.

"There are other works that are not as busy as you and we could do something there as well. But you shout the loudest: 'Dad, help!' But you know the truth: dad has nothing, he is a poor bitch [Milch uses the word 'Luder'], you are much richer. You say: 'We first want the money.' So that daddy also receives the bill. He is put under pressure because you say: 'If you do not send it, I'll steal, and then you'll go to jail.' Well, instead of looking after you, looking for savings, we have other work to do."

A lengthy argument ensued, with Kokothaki and Messerschmitt both defending the company's efforts and attempts to pursue the Me 262 development programme but it was clear that Messerschmitt AG was short-staffed to the point of being unable to meet its commitments.

In the meantime, the Probü was working with what scant resources were available on a more detailed design description for a high-altitude fighter, incorporating the aircraft shown in the June 26 report. The eventual outcome, on July 26, was a brochure entitled Vorschlag einer Höhenjägerentwicklung auf der Basis Me 109/Me 209 or 'Proposal for a high-altitude fighter on the basis of Me 109/Me 209'[14].

The introduction said: "In the following folder a proposal for a development series of high-altitude aircraft is presented in three stages. The subdivision of the development into several stages was chosen in order to develop a high-altitude fighter as quickly as possible and with as little expenditure of operating capacity and material as possible. In addition, this staging ensures that the increasing demands of the front line are met while the second and third stages are achieved in due time. The gradual development significantly reduces the testing risk compared to an immediate end-of-line solution with the DB 605.

"The first stage arises from the Me 109 G by changing only a few components and by introducing an intermediate wing section. These changes were kept to a minimum so that for the parts to be replaced are largely already structurally finished Me 209 components. A modification of the first stage is the installation of the DB 603 turbo in the DB 605, which causes only minor modifications to the engine on the fuselage side.

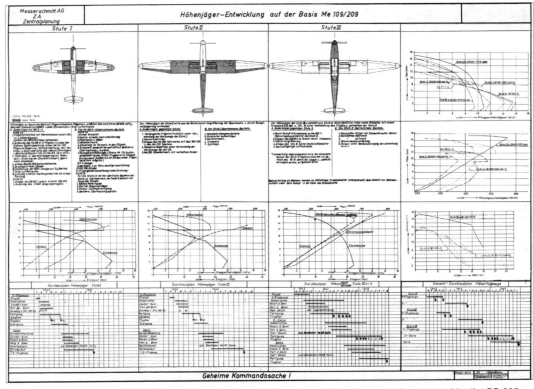

ABOVE: The three stages of P 1091 from the project report. Stage 1 and Stage 2 were to be powered by the DB 605 while the Stage 3 – the extreme high-altitude variant – had the DB 603 with TKL 15 turbosupercharger.

"The second stage has essentially only an increase in the wingspan with intermediate wing sections and a fuselage extension. In both cases, it is ensured that the existing tools are used. The engine is that of the first stage.

"The third stage will receive a new engine: the DB 603 with TKL 15. The engine is built as far as possible, from parts of the existing unit engine. Although the TKL 15 does not readily fit into the fuselage of the Stage 2 design, it is likely that this fuselage will be used, thickening the area around the TK 15 installation and cockpit to accommodate the lining for the exhaust and boost pipes. The third stage of development also meets the demand for a high-altitude bomber. In this case, the range is increased by installing additional fuel tanks in the wings and deleting the wing armament."

The Stage 1 design was labelled 'Me 109 H J' and was based on drawing III/483. The drawing included in the brochure bears the legend 'Höhenjäger 109 DB 605 und O2 Anlg.' and is signed by Hügelschäffer but another version of the drawing exists that is just labelled 'Me 109 H'. This would therefore appear to be simply the latest iteration of the Me 109 H with a 13.2m wingspan and 22.2m² wing area. The intermediate wing sections housed the aircraft's radiators and landing gear and even allowed space for extra fuel tanks. The outer wing was the normal Me 109 component.

The fuselage came from the Me 109 G-5 but with its armour removed and "possibly reinforced at some points to accommodate the forces from the enlarged rudder" from the Me 209. Controls came from the 109 with spacers for the wing sections. Undercarriage came from the G-5 too but with the struts extended by 20cm. The engine was also lifted from the G-5 but with an Me 210 propeller and the GM 1 injection system modified to operate with liquid oxygen instead of nitrous oxide. Armament was an MK 108 motor cannon and an MG 151 in each wing. Take-off weight was 3540kg.

Stage 2, shown in drawing III/484, was labelled 'P 1091 Höhenjäger mit DB 605 A + O2'. Compared to Stage 1, its wingspan was increased by 7.8m to 21m, with a corresponding area increase of 16.8m² to 39m². The front section of the fuselage was taken from the 109 but the rear section was extended by 2m. The tail and undercarriage came complete from the Me 209. The engine came from the Me 109 G but set 600mm further forward in the fuselage, with the addition of an intermediate engine carrier and correspondingly longer engine cowling. This newly created space could be used to house either extra fuel or liquid oxygen.

A propeller 3.4m in diameter was required and the radiators were "built into wing leading edge according to de Havilland Mosquito". Fuel and liquid oxygen capacity was the same as Stage 1. Weaponry was the same except with the option to swap the MG 151s for MK 108s. Take-off weight was 4410kg.

Stage 3 was the 'P 1091 Höhenjäger mit DB 603 A + TK 15', shown in drawing III/474 – the same drawing from the June 26 report. It had the same wings and wing radiators as Stage 2, a front fuselage section with pressure cabin from the Me 209, but modified as mentioned to suit the engine's external pipework. The tail and landing gear were again Me 209 parts. The DB 603 A with TKL 15 needed a six-bladed 4m diameter propeller and lacked the annular

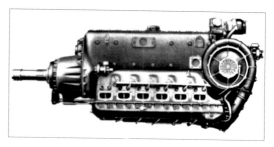

ABOVE: The Daimler-Benz DB 603 U was identified as the powerplant of choice for Messerschmitt's extreme high-altitude fighter at an early stage. This image shows the engine without its Hirth TKL 15 turbosupercharger.

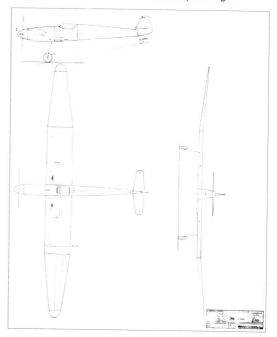

ABOVE: The P 1091 Stage 2, shown in Messerschmitt drawing III/484. The inner wings and rear fuselage were completely new but the forward fuselage and outer wings were retained from the Bf 109 G/Me 209. The tailplanes came from the Me 209. Stage 2 was dropped once Blohm & Voss became involved in the project.

radiator usually specified for the engine. Intercooling was to be replaced with methanol injection. Turbine air and oil cooling would be taken care of by a heat exchanger inside the engine's cowling. The exhaust gas turbocharger was positioned behind the fuel tank to the rear – hence the necessity of external pipes for carrying air to and from the engine up front.

The usual fuel tank was supplemented by an additional 225 litres of fuel and methanol in the mid-wing sections but weaponry was the same as Stage 2.

There was also a second version of Stage 3 – a Höhenbomber or 'high-altitude bomber'. The only differences were 830 litres of fuel and methanol in the wings rather than 225 plus a bomb rack under the right wing root capable of holding 250kg of munitions. Each of these three descriptions came with a little note attached which said: "The right to make changes to

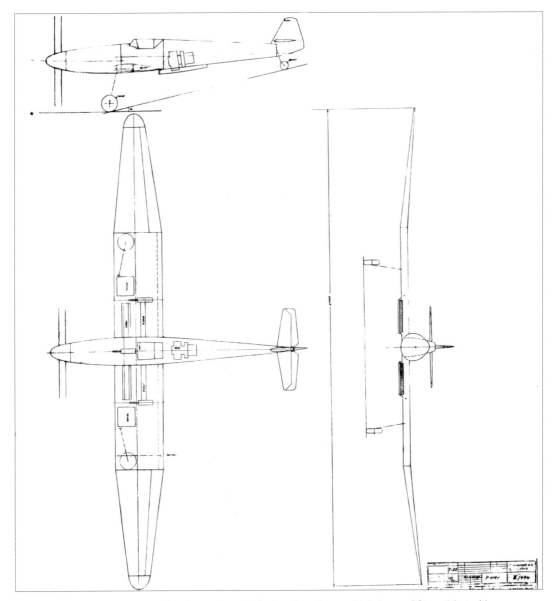

ABOVE: The third stage of P 1091 development was to feature the wings and tailplanes of Stage 2 but with a completely new fuselage. The DB 603 in the nose was connected to its TKL 15 turbosupercharger, behind the pilot, by tubes which ran beneath an outer skin, giving the fuselage a more bulbous appearance but leaving the surface smooth and unblemished.

the above short description, which may prove to be necessary with detailed processing, is reserved!"

On the same day, according to the Me 109 H Lebenslauf[15], written just 13 days later, Willy Messerschmitt met with Adolf Hitler and was verbally "given the task of developing a fighter-bomber from the Me 109, which was to rise higher than the enemy fighters with a 1000km range at high-altitude". Presumably Messerschmitt had handed the Vorschlag einer Höhenjägerentwicklung auf der Basis Me 109/Me 209 brochure to Hitler and the latter's preferred stage was the Höhenbomber.

A year after the 8-155 designation was originally applied, Messerschmitt had finally produced what may be regarded as the first version of the extreme high-altitude fighter that would eventually become the BV 155. The Stage 3 design from this document, the P 1091 Höhenjäger mit DB 603 A + TK 15 originally offered to the RLM on June 26, 1943, was the basis for everything that would follow.

HELP FROM BLOHM & VOSS

During a GL-Besprechung on August 3[16], the main topic up for discussion was the issue of productive capacity across the German aviation industry, without any representatives of that industry actually present. Milch turned his attention to which of the many aircraft types being built at that time the Luftwaffe could do without. He said: "Then comes the whole area of seaplanes. There is the question of what you can do. This goes back to Ar 196, which I do not judge as negative, but all the others, BV 138, 222, 238, I really want to kill off, Kleinrath [Generalmajor Kurt Kleinrath was on the Luftwaffe general staff], because in my opinion anyway nothing is going on with this heap of devices.

"I would like to give Vogt's entire office and his men to Messerschmitt to fill in the large hole that Messerschmitt's constructive capacity has. I prefer to do without these few aircraft. There come just one or two of them a month now. Whether we have the damned apparatus of ground personnel needed for these sea-things or not! What do they bring us? As good as nothing!"

The Me 109 H Lebenslauf explained that following Messerschmitt's meeting with Hitler it had been determined that the Höhenbomber was unachievable given existing engines and airframes. However, on the same day that Milch announced his plan to offer Blohm & Voss's resources up to Messerschmitt, Schwarz had met Willy Messerschmitt, Voigt and Hügelschäffer and given them an order, Protokol Nr. 500, for an experimental aircraft based on drawing III/482 – which apparently showed a Bf 109 G with minimal alterations to improve high-altitude performance. This was where the Bf 109 H diverged from the high-altitude fighter project – which would now need a new name.

On August 4, Oberst Georg Pasewaldt, head of the Technical Office's development department, broke the bad news to Blohm & Voss director Walter Blohm and Vogt that production of their trio of seaplanes had been cancelled and that the freed capacity must now be used to alleviate the burden on Messerschmitt. He sweetened the pill by suggesting that this might involve taking over partial responsibility for building the Me 262 – which seems to have gone a long way towards bringing Vogt on side.

At the next GL-Besprechung on August 13 a large section of the meeting was devoted to discussing how Blohm & Voss could help Messerschmitt[17]. Milch said: "What Blohm & Voss can give today in terms of designers

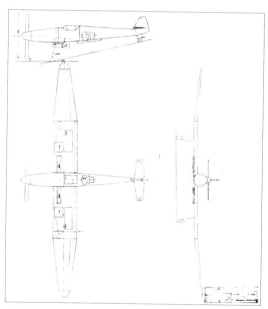

ABOVE: In addition to the P 1091 Stage 3 extreme high-altitude fighter, Messerschmitt also offered a bomber variant. At this point the company optimistically expected that a pair of wide but narrow under-wing radiators would be sufficient – an expectation soon to be confounded.

and workers should go in favour of Messerschmitt. Blohm & Voss is said to have only one stipulation on this issue: that Blohm & Voss should, if the war permits or requires, get their old men back as far as they want them.

"Under this condition Blohm & Voss would not only give up what they want to get rid of anyway, but also quite good people, also leading men, so that the old team spirit of Blohm & Voss is preserved and the later return is possible. Messerschmitt should not only fill his office with these people, but also get people who can approach work independently ... We have further discussed that Blohm & Voss ... is to take on a special task within the framework of Messerschmitt. We had talked about Vogt taking over all the fixture construction and preparation of the Me 262.

"Then we have just talked about the question that Messerschmitt, in addition to all other tasks, gets started very quickly in a new fighter, the 209, and for this extraordinary forces are needed. We are aware that Messerschmitt also has to develop a high-altitude variant, Stage 1, and later Stage 2. Whether you go straight to Stage 3 and skip Stage 2 or not, that's also an appointment matter and must be decided by Messerschmitt. Anyway, there are different stages of the high-altitude variant."

He said that whatever task Blohm & Voss was given, the priority was fighters and heavy fighters. Vogt told the meeting: "We are completely unencumbered and are ready to take over anything that the Messerschmitt company wishes to give. We have agreed and will do so. I still have quite a few people in Hamburg, then I have an intact wind tunnel and an experimental department where static tests can be made. All this can benefit the company. We can intervene to offer relief."

Messerschmitt said: "We have not talked in detail yet, but talked only briefly. But I am firmly convinced that we will work well together."

Milch said the details of which task Vogt was to take over did not need to be decided there and then – as long as the task given was within Blohm & Voss's capability to complete quickly. There was some discussion about the usage of Blohm & Voss's factories for building Messerschmitt fighters and Milch said he wasn't interested in how the details were arranged: "Today's question is how we can make the jump from 1000 fighters to 2000 fighters faster than initially planned. The other question is how, one day, we will make the leap in power and altitude and speed."

Messerschmitt was told he would initially get 700 men from Blohm & Voss but he replied: "Seven hundred is a drop in the bucket." Milch continued: "You also get 5000 and more. I want to give everything we get now, first and foremost to the fighters and heavy fighters, until that settles. Later we will again take care of the others, who are behind the fighter/heavy fighter programme. I expect to get about 70,000 German people by the end of this month. That's my promise ... This will primarily satisfy your company and Focke-Wulf again. The others have to wait a while."

Six days later 120 design engineers led by Vogt's assistant Pohlmann were already based at Messerschmitt's Augsburg headquarters, and had been assigned the task of developing the three-stage high-altitude fighter based on Vorschlag einer Höhenjägerentwicklung auf der Basis Me 109/Me 209.

Pohlmann sent Vogt a telex that day[18], which Willy Messerschmitt obtained a copy of, saying: "Have taken over as task all work on the extreme Höhenjäger Stage 3. Since this is actually a raw project, the task includes all static and aerodynamic work. In practical terms, this is a completely new model. This would include the construction and testing of five prototype aircraft, task is expected to run under emergency priority. Our prototyping capacity would be so busy. Secondary task for immediate employment of the designers: series production of the design documents – about 15,000 hours for Stage 1, also possibly serial documents for two-seat trainer aircraft.

"Messerschmitt asks if Blohm & Voss can take over the conversion of 30 Me 109s to trainers, about 1000 hours per aircraft. Most of the parts would be delivered. Delivery very urgent. It still has to be clarified whether our staff are conscripted for duty under Messerschmitt or have been merely assigned."

Hügelschäffer was sent a memo on August 23[19] requesting that all project documents on the 'Höhenjägers 109 H' be sent to Blohm & Voss by September 2 at the latest and on August 28 project P 1091 was formally transferred from Messerschmitt to Blohm & Voss. Less than two weeks later, on September 9, a meeting was held between Flugbaumeister Otto Malz, a senior staff engineer of the RLM's GL/C-E 2/III section, and representatives of both Blohm & Voss and Messerschmitt to decide how the project should proceed.

According to a Messerschmitt report written up the same day[20], it was "agreed that Höhenjäger Project Stage 3 will be fully developed by Blohm & Voss. Responsibility for development towards the RLM remains with Messerschmitt AG. A mandate was promised by Mr Malz. The type designation was determined to be Me 155 B [underlined]. Five prototype aircraft are to be built. The Höhenjäger Me 155 B arises from the Me 109 H and Me 109 G-5 through a series of changes, which are specified in the Project Transfer Mtt. AG to Blohm & Voss P 1091 of August 28, 1943 in detail and are binding for development.

"It is desirable to adopt as many existing components and assemblies as possible for the Me 155 B. As far as this is not possible, the existing resources 109 G-5 and 109 H are largely taken into account." All documents already created referring to the Me 109 H "now apply simultaneously to Me 155 B". All correspondence between Blohm & Voss and Messerschmitt AG was to be managed by the ZA-TL liaison department.

Blohm & Voss had been thrown in at the deep end. Stage 1 of the high-altitude fighter proposal of July 26 would remain with Messerschmitt as the Me 109 H but Blohm & Voss was given responsibility for building five prototypes of the long-winged extreme high-altitude Stage 3. Stage 2 became irrelevant. The RLM had allocated the Stage 3 project the designation Me 155 B – there never having been an 'A' – presumably because the type was, after a fashion, the successor to the project of 15 months earlier. With the agreement between the two companies now signed and sealed it was time to get to work. ●

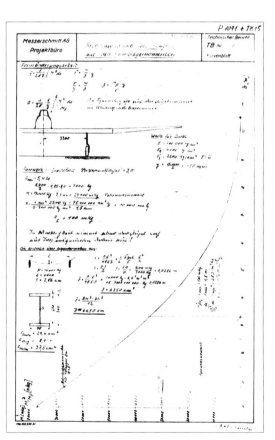

ABOVE: Messerschmitt Projektbüro sketch and calculations on the Me 155 B/P 1091 dated August 15, 1943 – shortly before the formal handover to Blohm & Voss.

Chapter 4
Split with Messerschmitt

September 1943 to February 1944 (Me 155 B and BV 155 B-1)

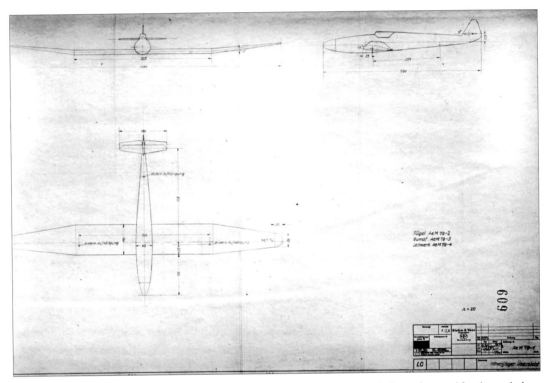

ABOVE: Blohm & Voss drew up designs for two high-altitude fighters with extremely long wings and fuselages during the autumn of 1943, had models built of each, and began a thorough programme of wind tunnel testing. This was the smaller of the two, depicted in drawing AeM 79-1, and clearly based on the P 1091.

September 10, 1943, saw Messerschmitt's Probü working on the Me 155 B's pressure cabin[1] – which was supposed to be capable of working up to an altitude of 17km. Unfortunately it had been determined that the Me 109 G's air compressor was "completely inadequate" for this. Possible solutions included the use of two compressors or use of air from the aircraft's engine, prior to methanol injection. A week later the question remained unresolved despite further investigation work.

Quite why Messerschmitt's projects office was working on the Me 155 B at all is unclear since in theory this work should now have been the sole responsibility of Blohm & Voss. Meanwhile, the latter had been closely examining Messerschmitt's initial concepts and working out how to turn them into a practical real-world aircraft. Among other queries, Vogt sent a telex to the Messerschmitt liaison office on September 22 to ask how many litres of fuel and methanol were to be carried by the high-altitude bomber version[2]. Probü project engineer Scherer wrote back the following day to tell him that the Höhenbomber had been designed to carry 1580 litres of fuel and methanol combined but that this was not an 'official' claim and new calculations would be needed to verify what was required[3].

Following this initial assessment period, Vogt wrote Messerschmitt a letter on October 5, 1943[4], listing problems identified in the original P 1091 Stage 3 concept and outlining Blohm & Voss's planned solutions. He said that the long narrow wings, as envisioned, lacked torsional rigidity; with the elimination of methanol injection, the radiator surface area required took up the entire inner wing section – making it impossible to accommodate the landing gear; the Me 209 tailplanes specified were too small in relation to the wings; and there were problems associated with the number of cut-outs necessary in the fuselage to attach an aerodynamic outer skin over the turbo feeder lines, which would run outside the normal 109 fuselage being used.

The first three problems had "led to the suggestion to build a box-shaped, exceptionally rigid wing support made of steel". This had the added advantage of reducing the number of fuel tanks from seven – one in the fuselage and three in each wing – to just three because in addition to the fuselage tank the steel wing supports could double up as fuel tanks. The weight saving would also allow for armour protection of the tanks.

No solution had yet been found for the radiator problem but Vogt tentatively suggested that the fuselage cut-outs issue could be resolved by simply leaving off the aerodynamic outer skin. He told Messerschmitt: "We have been reluctant to take such a step in terms of your own design tendency for purely aesthetic reasons." He asked for Messerschmitt's approval of the changes, saying: "We kindly ask you to let us know in due time in the second half of the month."

On October 12 Hügelschäffer and Voigt sent a telex to the Luftwaffe test centre at Rechlin concerning the necessary tyre sizes required for the Me 155 B[5]. They wanted to know what loads tyres measuring 770 x 270 could withstand and whether it was possible to develop a 790 x 235 tyre. The pair wrote to the RLM on the same day, saying that the standard fighter tyre size – 740 x 210 – was only barely adequate for the Me 155 B and asking for approval to switch to the new 790 x 235 size.

A week later Hügelschäffer wrote to Daimler-Benz asking for an update on the engine proposed for the Me 155 B since, up to this point the manufacturer had been somewhat vague about the 'DB 603 with TKL 15'[6].

He wrote: "Since we are currently completely unclear about the development of the TKL 15 (DVL-Hirth exhaust gas turbocharger 9-2279) now eligible in the engine DB 603, we ask you to give us the following information: 1) What is the name of this DB 603 variant with TKL 15 attachment? 2) What design differences does this engine variant have over DB 603 A or 603 E or DB 603 G? 3) What is the weight of this engine? 4) Does the performance of this engine without exhaust gas turbocharger correspond to the performance of the DB 603 A or DB 603 E or DB 603 G? 5) How much heat must be removed from the coolant and lubricant for this engine with TKL 15 fitted? For an immediate answer to these questions, we would be extremely grateful."

On October 20, Hügelschäffer and Voigt invited the Blohm & Voss Me 155 B project coordinators to Augsburg for a two-to-three day meeting about the aircraft on Tuesday, October 26, 1943, and also invited the RLM's Schwarz to be there too[7]. That same day,

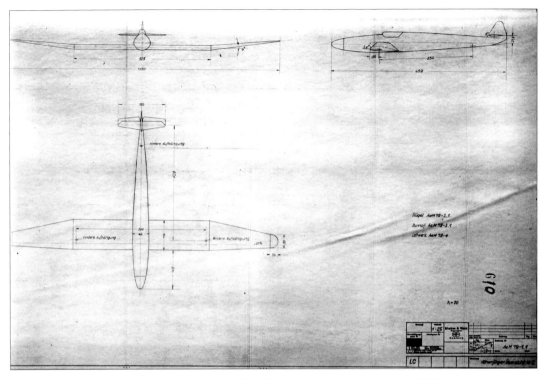

ABOVE: The second – even longer – Blohm & Voss Höhenjäger design, shown in drawing AeM 79-1.1.

Daimler-Benz replied to say that the DB 603 associated with the TKL 15 was in fact the 603 G model and Hügelschäffer noted in a memo[8] that "the calculations for the Me 155 B can therefore start with the known values". Rechlin also came back on the tyre size issue[9], promising to support the proposal for 790 x 235 tyres.

Hügelschäffer wrote to Blohm & Voss on October 25[10], asking that the project coordinators bring with them a copy of the original Vorschlag einer Höhenjägerentwicklung auf der Basis Me 109/Me 209 document and the calculations relating to their proposed new wing design. However, although the Blohm & Voss engineers turned up as requested, the meeting was cancelled at the last minute and rescheduled for November 11, this time at Messerschmitt's newly relocated project offices at Oberammergau[11].

Daimler-Benz director Fritz Nallinger wrote a summary of an internal company discussion concerning its work with Blohm & Voss on October 30, 1943, entitled Höhenjäger Me 155 bei Blohm & Voss[12]. He wrote: "The above machine is projected with DB 603 U and TKL 15 and was originally calculated to a peak altitude of 18km. Due to the weights calculated so far, however, only 16-16.5km will likely be reached."

He said the TKL 15 would be installed under the pilot's seat, meaning it was 3m from the engine. Exhaust and air ducts would run along the outside of the fuselage, half embedded in it. Intermediate and final air cooling would be by wet heat exchangers and there would be heat exchangers for the oil too in a system similar to that used on the Henschel Hs 130 A-0/ U6. The original 603 U, based on the 603 G, had been deleted from the RLM's development programme, so the 603 SS, based on the 603 A, would now be used instead. This would become the new 603 U and Nallinger noted that Blohm & Voss had urged his company to send over a definitive drawing of it. The associated propeller would be a six-bladed unit.

PARTNERSHIP IN JEOPARDY

Meanwhile, the Messerschmitt Probü had drafted a list of 41 "discussion points" for the November 11 meeting – which in fact amounted to a series of instructions for the Blohm & Voss team[13]. These included: "The outer wing is expediently not to be taken up from Me 209, but from Me 109 H [work on which was progressing separately]" and "Move the TKL 15 unit installation far back enough so that a second man can be accommodated in accordance with the arrangement in the Me 109 trainer [Blohm & Voss was now converting Bf 109s into two-seat trainers in addition to its other Messerschmitt-related tasks]"; "The main landing gear receives the wheels 770 x 270", "Reproduce the water-methanol injection according to the latest documents available from DB"; "The gyroscopic moments of propeller and TKL 15 when spinning must be taken into account," and so on.

Unfortunately, the Blohm & Voss team were not told that the meeting had been relocated as well as being rescheduled and turned up at Augsburg, only to then be forced to travel down to Oberammergau. Having already been messed around they did not take kindly to the Probü's lengthy list of instructions. As soon as the meeting ended, they communicated their displeasure to Vogt who then rang the RLM's development department to complain.

On November 17, 1943, the RLM's C-E 2 department sent Messerschmitt a strongly-worded note of reproof with the subject line 'Me 155 B'[14] which said: "Investigations planned by you, Messerschmitt AG, with regard to armament reinforcement and the arrangement of a second seat are not required by the Technical Office. This work must be stopped immediately. If it proves necessary that in addition to the intentionally lightly-built extreme Höhenjäger a heavy fighter is required, it will probably be designed on the two-engine basis. Decisive for the design of the aircraft are still the requirements issued by the Technical Office".

And the following day the same department sent Messerschmitt another note[15], this time saying: "GL/C-E [Major Siegfried Knemeyer, who had replaced Pasewaldt as head of the Technical Office's development department] has learned from the developmental team at Blohm & Voss that you have submitted to the company Blohm & Voss new requirements for the special high-altitude fighter, which definitely cannot contribute to a well-grounded project and would make it unsuitable for its intended purpose.

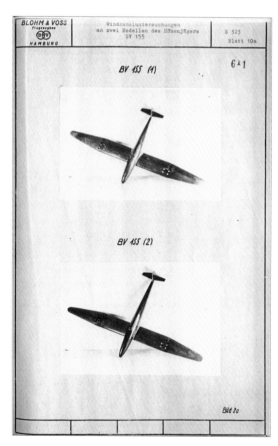

ABOVE: Wind tunnel models of the two Blohm & Voss Höhenjägers. Although the drawings and models were prepared in late 1943, the actual report on results was not published until April 14, 1944.

"You are asked not to bother the company Blohm & Voss in their work by unnecessary demands and investigations, especially as new demands for the project were not announced by GL/C-E."

The Messerschmitt team, who had been working diligently to help their Blohm & Voss colleagues up to this point, were apparently taken aback by this before resolving to waste no more of their own time on the Me 155 B. On November 24, 1943, Hügelschäffer issued a memo to the Probü staff[16] saying: "Working hours should in general no longer be spent on the Me 155 B since the project office is fully occupied with other work. The project was reallocated to Blohm and Voss for this reason.

"Of course, the requirement that no hours of work should be used to any substantial extent also means that the involvement of the Messerschmitt project office is now restricted to a pure technical management responsibility. The treatment of Me 155 B should be as follows: Blohm & Voss put the finished work to us at certain intervals for discussion and decision. It is then decided here in cooperation with Blohm & Voss, which of the solutions presented are selected.

"If further work is needed to make these decisions, such as investigations on radiator installation, propeller performance calculations or also design, this work will be carried out in Oberammergau with workers to be provided by Blohm & Voss. Orders for Me 155 B processing in the project office are generally blocked. If necessary, release can be made on a case-by-case basis for a limited amount of time and for limited hours by me."

Blohm & Voss, meanwhile, was not devoting as much effort to the Me 155 B as it might have been. Vogt wrote a letter to the RLM on November 29[17] saying that design drawings and calculations for the P 186 glide-fighter would take about 10,000 hours to complete and that "this work can only be carried out informally during the start-up period of the construction of the Höhenjäger Me 155, that is, now. Then the drawings can be delivered at the end of February. If the production could be started immediately, the possible flight schedule would fall on the turn of the month in March/April".

Work on the tiny P 186, soon to be redesignated BV 40, had begun in August 1943[18]. It was a heavily armoured but unpowered aircraft designed to be towed aloft behind an ordinary fighter before being released above an enemy bomber formation to then swoop down and carry out its attack. While the B&V team never stopped working on other projects, the BV 40 rapidly reached the prototype stage of development and began to consume a

Höhenjäger

Baubeschreibung

(B&V)

BLOHM & VOSS · FLUGZEUGBAU · HAMBURG

JANUAR 1944

ABOVE: The cover of Blohm & Voss's first and only major report on the Me 155 B under that designation, dated January 1944. Evidence suggests it was delivered to the RLM during the first few days of the month.

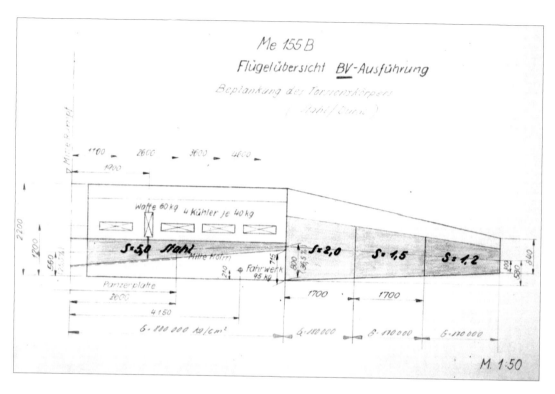

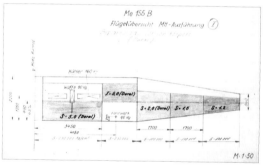

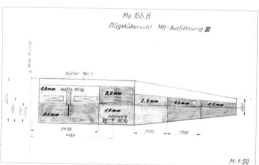

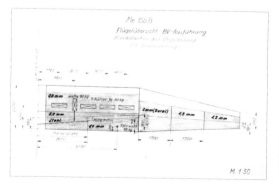

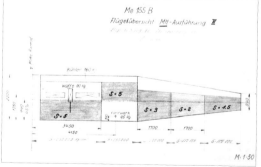

ABOVE: The differing wing designs of Messerschmitt and Blohm & Voss as both companies sought a solution to the problem of too many heavy wing radiators. These come from a document which may be loosely dated to the second week of November 1943 – shortly before relations between the two firms soured.

significant amount of time and resources. Its development would continue to run in parallel with that of the Me 155 B/BV 155 into November 1944.

Also on November 29, 1943, Vogt called his team together for the first formal design review of the 'Me 155 B-1'[19] – the earliest known use of the '-1' in period documents. Up for discussion were the centre of gravity and attachment points for the wings which allowed "both the old Me 109 and the new B&V wing to be attached". In accordance with the discussions at Oberammergau on the 11th the outer wings were now to be sourced from the Bf 109 G-5 rather than the Me 209 and the form of the aircraft's radiators was still a work in progress. The wing-mounted weapons had now been moved so far outwards that a propeller diameter of 4.05m was possible and investigations were being undertaken with regard to the motor cannon installation.

In the minutes of the meeting it is noted that "the TKL 15 remains in position. The second crewman is not taken into account". Finally, it was noted that the first Me 155 B prototype would have an entirely new tail unit with a tailplane surface area of 4m² but it was still intended that the production model would use the Me 209 tail because "extension of the old Me 209 tail has to be possible". Workshop drawings for this were to be drafted in Paris.

Evidently the relationship between Blohm & Voss and Messerschmitt continued to be somewhat fragile and wheels were turning behind the scenes which would soon break it apart.

Messerschmitt managing director Kokothaki had by now been made aware of the notes sent to his company by the C-E 2 and wasn't very happy about them. He wrote to the Blohm & Voss liaison officer Bley on December 1[20]: "To my knowledge, Blohm & Voss direct or through us, in agreement with the Technical Office, has received an order for development of an extreme high-altitude fighter, with the special requirement that as many parts of an existing fighter be carried over as possible.

"As far as I know, Messerschmitt has taken over the technical responsibility for this aircraft. Now the RLM writes in a letter or telex that we make demands on the project, which would worsen the project, and inform us directly that Blohm & Voss should not be influenced. Therefore, I ask you to clarify with the authorities in the RLM whether

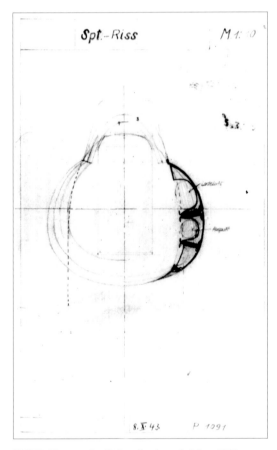

ABOVE: Messerschmitt drawing from October 1943 showing how the pipework transferring air to and from the Hirth turbosupercharger was to be hidden beneath a streamlined outer skin attached to the original Bf 109 G fuselage. Blohm & Voss believed that the cut-outs required would be too troublesome and suggested simply leaving the skin off.

should continue to have the technical responsibility for this project, according to the aforementioned guidelines."

He said that if the RLM could not allow Messerschmitt to retain sole technical responsibility for the project then "we are forced to withdraw from working with Blohm & Voss. It is not acceptable for us to assume the technical responsibility and then receive direct instructions from the RLM which undermine the authority that is necessary for the performance of the task".

On December 3, Oberammergau wrote to Blohm & Voss[21] to remind them that the outer wings of the Me 155 B were to be taken over from the Bf 109 H – "we point out that for the prototype Me 155 B, Me 209 wings are not available!"

The second Blohm & Voss-led construction review for the Me 155 B was on December 7[22]. It was now decided that Me 209 tail surfaces would no longer be considered because only a 4m² surface area would do. The rear fuselage of the aircraft correspondingly now needed to be strengthened to account for the enlarged tail planes. Test fittings of how the TKL 15 would be installed in the fuselage needed to be speeded up.

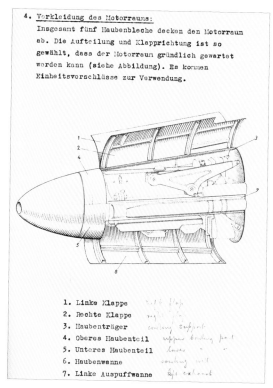

4. Verkleidung des Motorraums:
Insgesamt fünf Haubenbleche decken den Motorraum ab. Die Aufteilung und Klapprichtung ist so gewählt, dass der Motorraum gründlich gewartet werden kann (siehe Abbildung). Es kommen Einheitsverschlüsse zur Verwendung.

1. Linke Klappe
2. Rechte Klappe
3. Haubenträger
4. Oberes Haubenteil
5. Unteres Haubenteil
6. Haubenwanne
7. Linke Auspuffwanne

ABOVE: The Me 155's DB 603 U engine was to be covered with five panels designed to allow technicians the best possible access for servicing.

The undercarriage would have hydraulic retraction and a mechanical lock when retracted that was independent of the hydraulics. The lock would incorporate an emergency release and a hand pump system for the hydraulics was to be installed for emergencies.

The aircraft's armament was one MK 108 and two MG 151/20s but "the installation of an MK 103 in the fuselage must be possible. However, the installation of the MK 108 and possibly also the MK 103 in the wing still has to be provided by us".

Vogt noted that the Technical Office had set a deadline of December 15 for a short description of the reworked project, based on Blohm & Voss's amendments, which had to set out how the performance of the Blohm & Voss version differed from those originally provided by Messerschmitt.

CRITICISING MESSERSCHMITT

Willy Messerschmitt himself wrote a note to the company liaison office on December 8 headed "Me 109 H series production"[23] which said: "Making the Me 109 H ready for series production, namely fuselage, outer wing, undercarriage, tail, engine and equipment at Messerschmitt AG Oberammergau, with intermediate wing by Blohm & Voss, has the highest priority. The work of Blohm & Voss will be overseen by our structural department. The reason for the current determination that, contrary to the earlier agreement, mass production of the aircraft is largely made here, is because no dates have been agreed with Blohm & Voss yet, so that there the work has hardly begun."

Vogt's third formal Me 155 B-1 design review took place less than a week after the second, on December 13[24]. The gathered Blohm & Voss staff heard that "after a detailed discussion between Behrmann [Albert Behrmann of Blohm & Voss] and Dr [Kurt] Frey (Messerschmitt) a four-bladed wood-blade propeller has been decided upon. Diameter 3.7m, weight supposedly 290kg (has to be checked!). Delivery date June 1944". This was a lighter prop than the six-bladed one originally planned, necessitating a shift in the aircraft's centre of gravity to the rear – which meant that the wing had to be moved 30mm further back.

A visit by Heinrich Beauvais and Klein from the Luftwaffe's Rechlin test centre had "given rise to various reservations about the use of the Me 109 cockpit (poor visibility to the rear, too narrow for pressure suit, probably not sufficiently pressure-tight). But there is a lot to be said for the maintenance of the old cockpits, not least the assurances of Messerschmitt that the new pressure cabin of the Me 109 K will be in order".

Construction of the aircraft's tail would be carried out under contract in Paris but the Me 209 tailwheel arrangement for the first prototype would have to become a special order item "because the Me 209 will probably not be built".

On December 15, the Blohm & Voss/Messerschmitt liaison office wrote to the RLM requesting that the aircraft's official designation be changed from Me 155 B to Me 155 B-1 and the then-current state of the aircraft was embodied in drawing 8-155.00-11[25].

The fourth design review was on December 20[26] and it was reported that maximum take-off weight had been recalculated but remained the same at 5600kg. Theoretical work on the wing radiators had indicated that a single taller, narrower radiator would be better than several broad low profile ones. And it had been left to Messerschmitt to clarify what should be done about the engine carrying framework and tailwheel now that the Me 209 was not going to be built.

The Me 209 had always been a problematic aircraft for the Me 155 B to share components with because there was simply no capacity available to design or build it. Messerschmitt had produced a short description of an Me 209 H with DB 627 engine on October 25[27] but at an Entwicklungsbesprechung on October 29, 1943[28], there was growing opposition to the Me 209. Knemeyer called for it to be cancelled outright. Two further descriptions had been produced on November 29 – for an Me 209 with Jumo 213 E[29] and an Me 209 H with Jumo 213 E[30] – but the whole programme was finally cancelled in mid-December.

In early January 1944, more than a fortnight late, Blohm & Voss delivered the short description required by the RLM with the rather long-winded title Höhenjäger für 15 bis 16km Arbeitshöhe mit Triebwerk DB 603 und Turbolader TK 15 (although the front cover simply said 'Höhenjäger Baubeschreibung'), based on drawing 8-155.00-11[31]. The description certainly fulfilled its remit of explaining how the performance of the B&V version of the 155 differed from that of the Messerschmitt version but it went further – criticising almost every aspect of the original design.

The introduction began: "The documents handed over by Messrs. Messerschmitt AG, Augsburg, during the month of August forced us, at the end of detailed considerations, to a fundamental transformation of the most essential components, namely: the static structure of the inner wing; fuel storage; undercarriage size and placement; the cooling system; the profile shape of the wing; the installation of the turbocharger system and the tail unit."

OPPOSITE: The earliest known version of the post-P 1091 Me 155 B-1 as it appeared in Blohm & Voss's January 1944 report. This was drawing 8-155.00-11 and already embodies a substantial changes to Messerschmitt's preliminary designs.

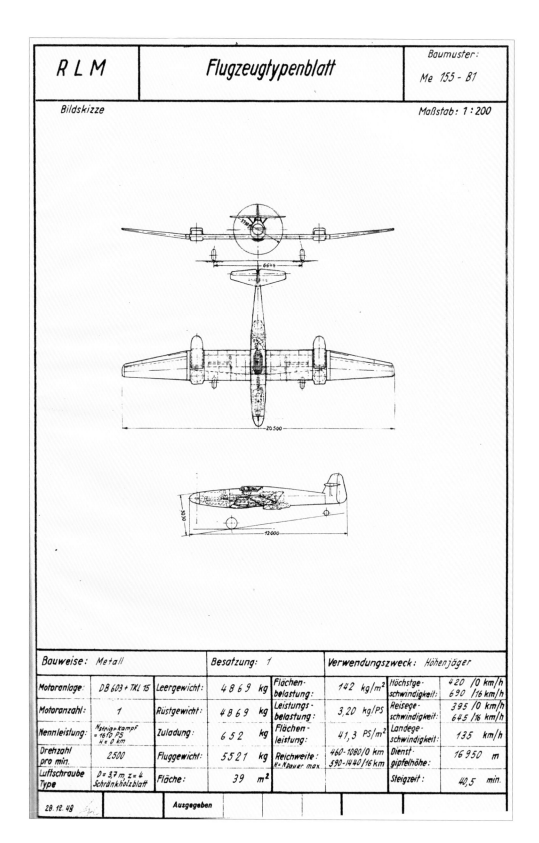

RLM	Flugzeugtypenblatt	Baumuster: Me 155 - B1

Bildskizze

Maßstab: 1 : 200

Bauweise: Metall		Besatzung: 1			Verwendungszweck: Höhenjäger	
Motoranlage:	DB 603 + TKL 15	Leergewicht:	4869 kg	Flächen-belastung:	142 kg/m²	Höchstge-schwindigkeit:	420 /0 km/h 690 /16 km/h
Motoranzahl:	1	Rüstgewicht:	4869 kg	Leistungs-belastung:	3,20 kg/PS	Reisege-schwindigkeit:	395 /0 km/h 645 /16 km/h
Nennleistung:	Nsteig+kampf = 1610 PS H = 0 km	Zuladung:	652 kg	Flächen-leistung:	41,3 PS/m²	Landege-schwindigkeit:	135 km/h
Drehzahl pro min.	2500	Fluggewicht:	5521 kg	Reichweite: H = Ndauer max	460-1080/0 km 590-1440/16 km	Dienst-gipfelhöhe:	16950 m
Luftschraube Type	D = 3,7 m, z = 4 Schränkholzblatt	Fläche:	39 m²			Steigzeit:	40,5 min.

28. 12. 49		Ausgegeben					

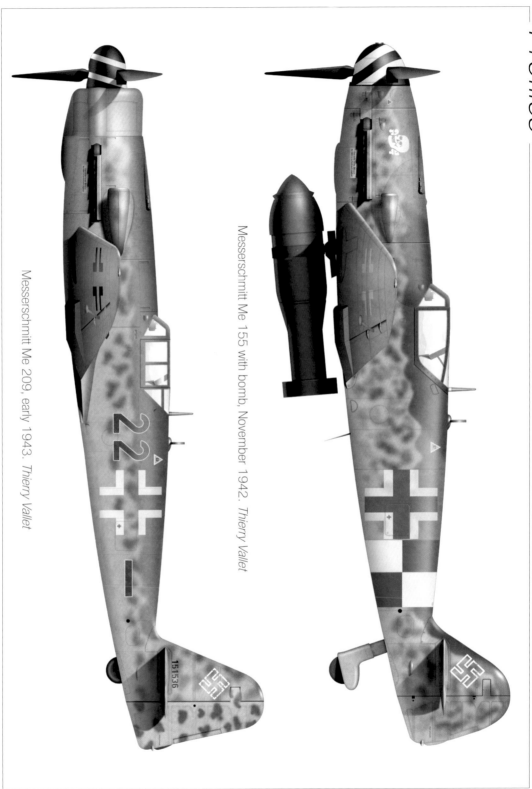

Messerschmitt Me 155 with bomb, November 1942. *Thierry Vallet*

Messerschmitt Me 209, early 1943. *Thierry Vallet*

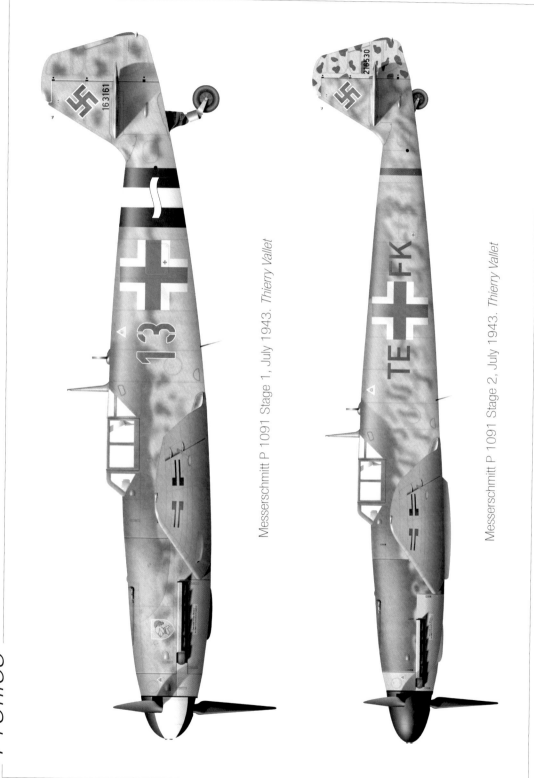

Messerschmitt P 1091 Stage 1, July 1943. *Thierry Vallet*

Messerschmitt P 1091 Stage 2, July 1943. *Thierry Vallet*

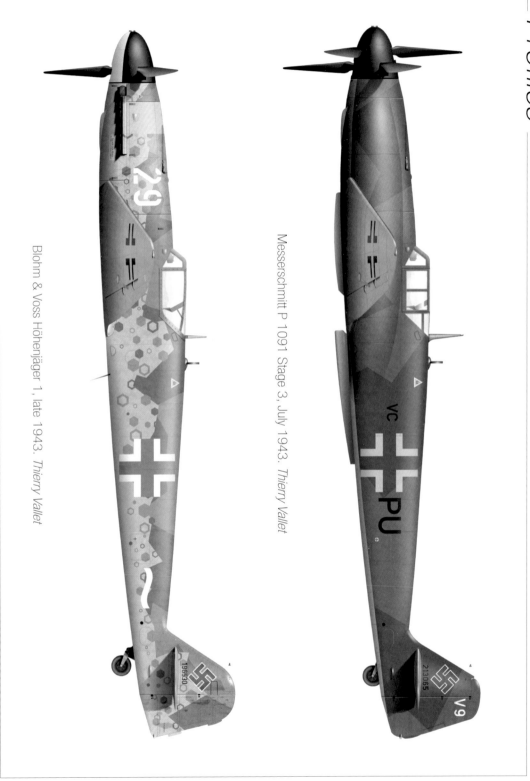

Profiles

Messerschmitt P 1091 Stage 3, July 1943. *Thierry Vallet*

Blohm & Voss Höhenjäger 1, late 1943. *Thierry Vallet*

50

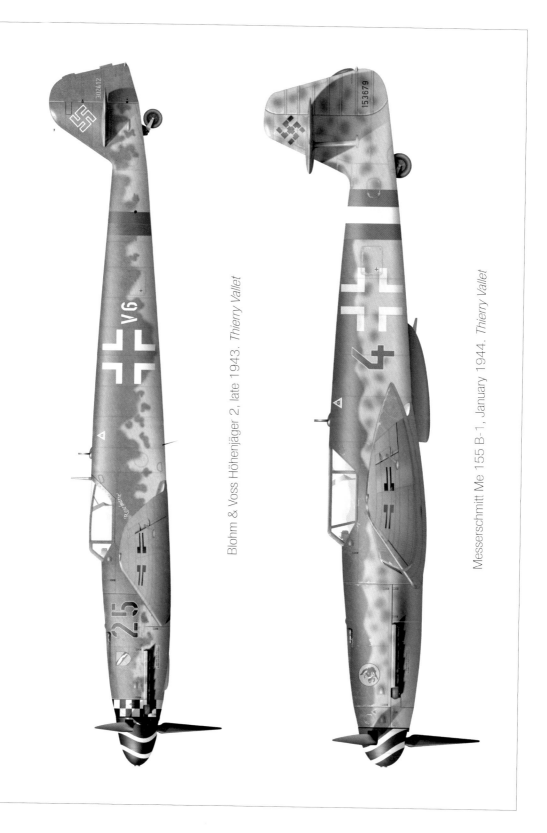

Blohm & Voss Höhenjäger 2, late 1943. *Thierry Vallet*

Messerschmitt Me 155 B-1, January 1944. *Thierry Vallet*

Profiles

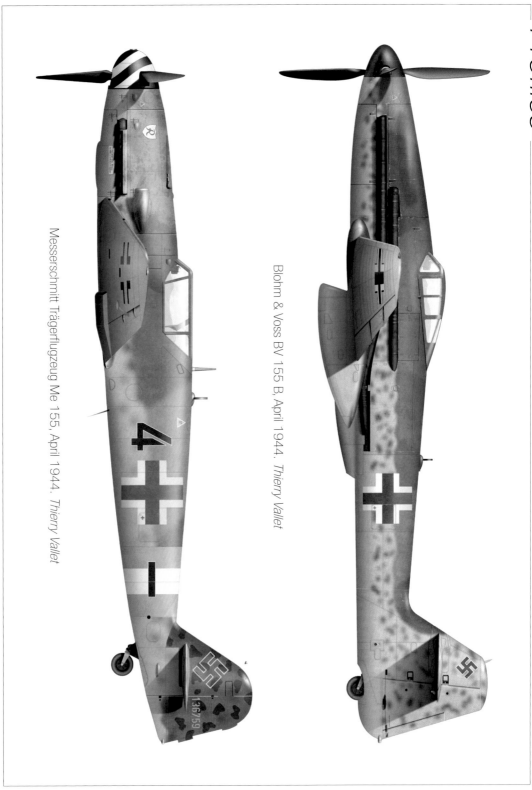

Messerschmitt Trägerflugzeug Me 155, April 1944. *Thierry Vallet*

Blohm & Voss BV 155 B, April 1944. *Thierry Vallet*

B&V 155 front view
+ B&V 155 Top View
Blohm & Voss BV 155 B,
April 1944.
Thierry Vallet

Profiles

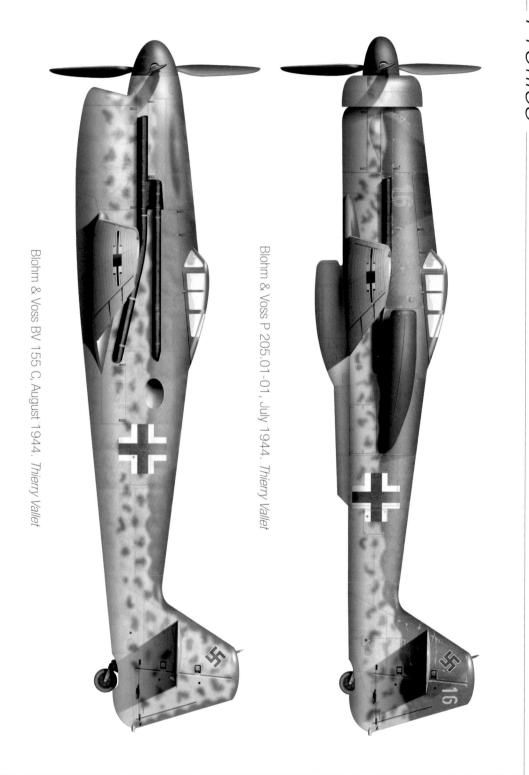

Blohm & Voss BV 155 C, August 1944. *Thierry Vallet*

Blohm & Voss P 205.01-01, July 1944. *Thierry Vallet*

The Messerschmitt-designed wings were not only too heavy and lacking in rigidity, but "such a wing on a high-altitude fighter of large span would be dangerous, not to say impossible". The new B&V wing was the one Vogt had outlined to Messerschmitt in his letter of October 5. There had been "arguments with the company Messerschmitt about the wheel size" which failed to reach a consensus, but based on RLM guidelines B&V had "opted for a sufficiently large wheel, which led to a local bulging of the wing. But we have merged this bulge with the radiator housing in the interest of least total disturbance".

Calculations had shown that very large radiator surfaces were needed and Messerschmitt's intended solution of placing eight low-profile radiators behind the wing spar "turned out to be particularly unfortunate", involving lots of pipework which would be sensitive to battle damage – not to mention individual control of each radiator being impractical.

The Blohm & Voss solution was to combined the smaller radiators into a single radiator housing on each wing where the necessary surface area was obtained by placing the radiator itself at an angle within the housing. Positioned behind the steel wing box structure it was better protected from fire incoming from the front. For the inner wing a laminar profile similar to that of the P-51 Mustang was chosen even though this was "deviating from Messerschmitt, who wanted us to try and get along without changing the profile".

The outer wing "can be profiled without reference to the inner wing at the boundary surface due to the radiator. So you could also use the wing of the Me 109, for example", although even this would require various changes such as changing the aileron and covering the undercarriage cutout "so there is so little left of the original wing that it makes more sense to simply build a new wing".

Messerschmitt's plan to cover over the fuselage turbocharger ducting "could not be met" so it was left exposed but partially sunk into the fuselage, which would make it much easier to access for maintenance and repair. And the idea of using the tailplane of an existing aircraft for the 155 was deemed ridiculous: "We could not convince ourselves that one would have to get along with an otherwise nearly doubled aircraft but with an unchanged tail.

"The proportion of the tailplane in relation to the wing area fell to a value that would be far below what has ever been flown before (about 7%). This risk seemed quite absurd for an extremely high-altitude craft, which by nature requires considerably

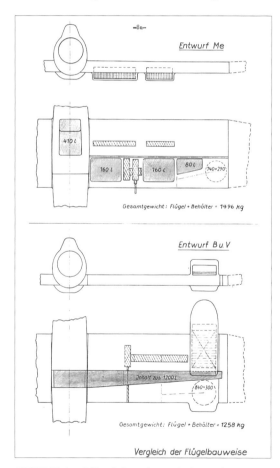

ABOVE: Blohm & Voss's ingenious solution to the Me 155's wing radiator problem is illustrated in this diagram from the January 1944 report. It was thought that fitting a large radiator diagonally inside a single nacelle would provide the same cooling as fitting smaller radiators vertically inside several nacelles.

more from the pilot than a regular aeroplane. For high-altitude flight you should strive for a particularly benevolent, stable behaviour."

Blohm & Voss regarded their new 4m² tailplane, increased from the Me 209's standard 2.8m², as the minimum size possible. The new Me 155 B-1 had a wingspan of 20.5m, 50cm shorter than that of the P 1091 Stage 3 fighter, but its fuselage was 12m long compared to 11.72m for the P 1091. Wing area was 39m², the same as the P 1091, and take-off weight was now 5521kg – an increase of 76kg.

There were four different weapons options: an MK 108 motor cannon and two MG 151/20s in the wings; an MK 103 and two MG 151/15 Es; an MK 108 and two more MK 108s in the wings, and an MK 103 plus two more MK 103s in the wings. In each case the Revi 16 B gunsight was specified.

BLOHM & VOSS ALONE

The fifth design review was held on January 4, 1944[32], and it was decided that the aircraft's tail structure would be wooden, with the question of whether the tailplanes could be covered with fabric to save weight. Dimensions for the propeller spinner were urgently needed and progress was being made on points concerning jacking up, hoisting, towing, anchoring and lifting of the aircraft. Construction schedules were now being drawn up.

The sixth review, on January 10[33], heard that due to the extra weight and "because of other concerns that have been raised regarding the preservation of timber construction" it was decided that the Me 155 B's tail would be made from Duralumin – but with the tailplanes skinned in fabric. Workshop drawings for the outer wings were being made in Paris and were expected to be ready by mid-February. The bespoke undercarriage would be supplied complete by Kronprinz "except for the mechanism of the main landing gear, which we have to procure ourselves".

Five days later, the RLM's Technical Office issued a memo approving the designation change requested exactly a month earlier[34], from 8-155 B to 8-155 B-1.

A delegation from Blohm & Voss visited Junkers' Dessau headquarters on a two-day fact-finding mission from January 19-20 to learn about that company's work on pressure cabins and high-altitude flight.

The precise point at which Blohm & Voss assumed sole responsibility for development of the 155 B-1 is unclear. However, a meeting was held on January 20 at Lechfeld specifically to discuss staff issues relating to the Me 262 programme[35]. The Messerschmitt high-performance twin-jet single seat aircraft was urgently needed for the Luftwaffe and the RLM wanted to scrape together whatever additional resources might be available across the German aviation industry to help expedite it.

According to the minutes, part-way through the meeting the unnamed Messerschmitt representative mentioned that 600 skilled worked were still on loan from Blohm & Voss to Messerschmitt at Augsburg and were working exclusively on the Me 262. Milch said that the workers were supposed to be working on the 262 at Blohm & Voss's premises. Oberstleutnant Ulrich Diesing, the new head of the Luftwaffe Planning Office, said that Blohm & Voss had applied for the workers to be returned but this had not happened yet.

The Messerschmitt representative said: "I must point out that the claim of Blohm & Voss will be raised after the meeting." Milch replied: "The Blohm & Voss question is specially examined. For the time being, keep the people until a directive has been issued. We do not need to talk about this question today."

While much of that exchange clearly refers to the allocation of workers, the fact that "the Blohm & Voss question is specially examined" suggests that the wider picture of the ongoing relationship between Messerschmitt and Blohm & Voss was being reviewed by the RLM at this point.

The first "construction review" of the Me 155 B-1, as opposed to a design review, took place on February 3[36]. Top of the agenda was the type's radiator and it was reported that Dr Dietrich Küchemann of the Aerodynamiche Versuchsanstalt (AVA) in Göttingen had proposed repositioning the aircraft's radiators to the underside of its wings but this redesign "will be deferred until the tests with the previous arrangement have been completed". Within a month, this change would be made.

The meeting also heard that there was fresh information available about the shape and dimensions of the air intake channel for the TKL 15 – positioned under the fuselage – and that the cockpit roof would have to be raised by 80mm due to the proposed gunsight installation.

At the next construction review just two days later[37] there was some discussion about how to build the tailplane without supporting struts and it was decided that it should be lowered by 150mm. This was the last Blohm & Voss conference to mention the Me 155 B-1 and the minutes of the following meeting on February 10, 1944, are headed Konstruktionsbesprechung BV 155[38] – Messerschmitt was now out of the picture and henceforth Blohm & Voss was fully in control of the type's development. ●

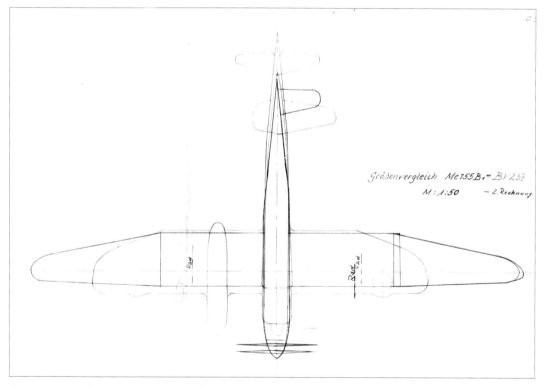

Größenvergleich Me155B₁ = BV 237
M : 1:50   – 2. Rechnung

ABOVE: Blohm & Voss drawing comparing the size of the Me 155 B-1 with that of the BV 237 – an asymmetrical aircraft designed as a replacement for the Ju 87 Stuka. Blohm & Voss designed a staggering number of aircraft during the war and even as work progressed on the Me 155 the company continued to spread its resources across numerous different projects. There is no date on the drawing but fact that it features the Me 155 B-1 places it somewhere between November 29, 1943, and February 10, 1944.

Chapter 5
Back from the brink
February 1944 to January 1945
(BV 155 B-1 to BV 155 C)

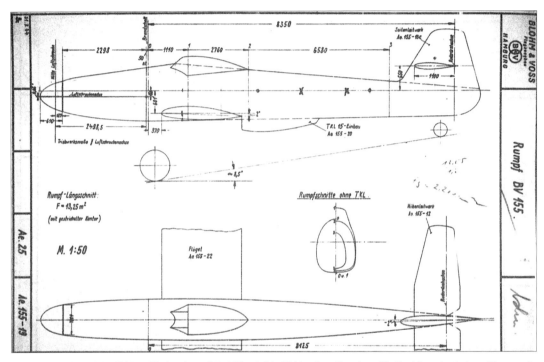

ABOVE: Drawing of the BV 155 B's fuselage dated March 31, 1944, when the aircraft's final form had almost been set.

The first BV 155 construction review heard model tests on the radiator's intake were ongoing, the upper part of the tailfin was designed to be removable and the tailwheel would not retract fully, with 80mm remaining outside the contour of the fuselage and "cover flaps are not provided". The meeting heard that the workshop had urgently requested information about the type's equipment.

Five days later the next review[1] was told that the aircraft's weight had risen 79kg to 5600kg but the main "purpose of the meeting was to bring about a clarification concerning the delivery of the drawing documents necessary for the equipment construction. The pre-clearing of the BV 155 is unfortunately not yet fully completed, so that e.g. information about the fuselage drawing deliveries can only be made available in about eight days".

However, the inner wing drawings were ready and the outer wing drawings would be ready on February 23. The engine cowling drawings would be available on February 29 but there was no fixed date for the tail unit.

Armour was discussed at a meeting on February 21[2] and a decision on this point was due to be taken at a meeting at Rechlin the following day. The issue of deleting the tailplane support struts re-emerged and the type's calculated landing speed was being checked and compared against other models. Leading edge flaps would not be provided on the BV 155 B-1 V1. Finally, "all agreed that a mock-up is needed" and arrangements for this were being made.

The review on March 9[3] heard that a test mock-up of the entire front section of the aircraft was being constructed to clarify welding and strength issues. Drawings and documents were available for this section, as were drawings for the fuselage mid-section apart from the framework that would hold the turbocharger. The general structure of the rear fuselage was fully designed apart from the connection points for the tail.

The following day a meeting discussed the BV 155's controls and the "ambiguity" surrounding the state of the tail was causing difficulties in the laying of control cables[4]. Similarly, the cables in the wings were said to be uncomfortably close to the aircraft's weapons. The aircraft's radio equipment positioning had been confirmed but the position of their antennae needed to be clarified. Both landing lights and pitot tube were to be installed in the outer wings. Fitting the MK 103 would be difficult because it weighed 150kg and there was concern about the ammunition box for the motor cannon being heated by air moving through the engine system.

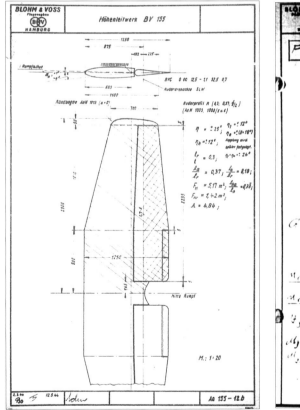
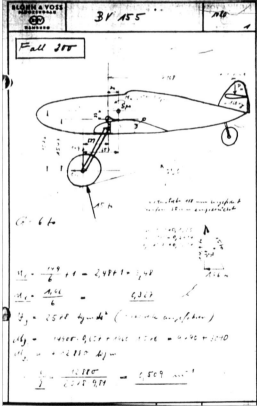

ABOVE LEFT: The BV 155 B tail plane as shown in a drawing dated March 3, 1944. Messerschmitt had originally planned to give the Me 155 standard Me 209 tailplanes but with Blohm & Voss in charge a larger bespoke component was specified. ABOVE RIGHT: This undated sketch comes from a book containing several dozen pages of sketches and calculations concerning the BV 155's undercarriage and is believe to date from the spring of 1944.

The engine installation was the main topic for discussion at the March 11 construction review[5]. The engine carrier supplied by Daimler-Benz had been found to be 50mm longer than intended but all this meant was that the connection fittings on the fuselage had had to be correspondingly altered. Questions were raised about the Knorr compressor for the pressure cabin and it was noted that the aircraft's lubricant reservoir in front of the engine was designed for a fuel supply of 1200 litres. If more fuel was to be carried in the wings an additional lubricant tank would be needed.

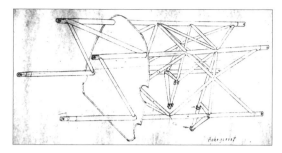

ABOVE: A drawing showing the tubular structure of the BV 155 B's fuselage frame.

The arrangement of the turbocharger's air feed pipe was finalised and the final positions of the exhaust pipes were to be determined the following week. Drag of the external cooling system of the aircraft was being measured by Daimler-Benz – B&V having delivered the necessary pipework.

The hydraulic system had also been finalised and the most suitable structural locations for the attachment of drop tanks were being determined.

The construction review on the 14th[6] heard that the workshop was having difficulties in manufacturing the steel box wing spars. Drawings for the undercarriage were now with the workshop and the weapons installation was going as planned.

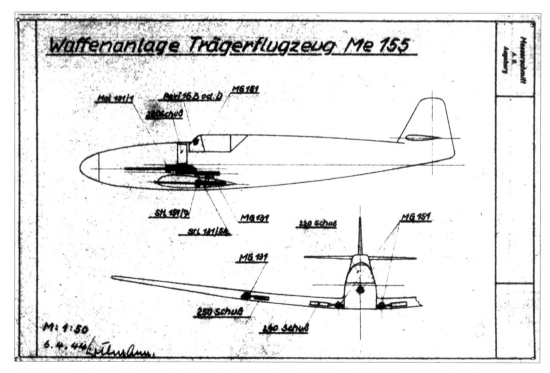

ABOVE: Even as Blohm & Voss was finalising the design of the BV 155, in April 1944 Messerschmitt produced a document detailing different armament layouts for its then-current designs and included this drawing of the 'Me 155' carrier aircraft.

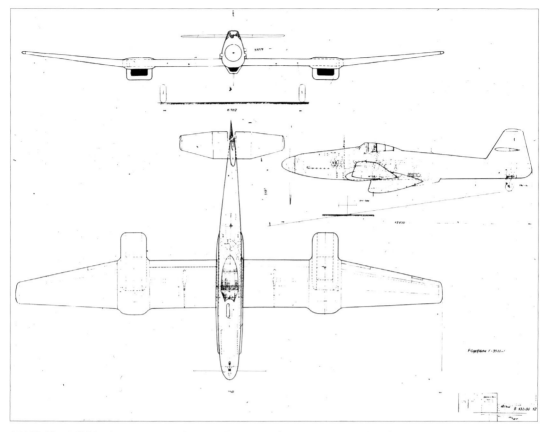

ABOVE: The definitive BV 155 B layout is shown in this drawing – 8-155.00-12 of April 19, 1944. Blohm & Voss based its calculations for the aircraft on the design depicted here.

The spar structure of the outer wings was going to be similar to that of the Me 262 – Blohm & Voss having now learned all about this from its experiences of working with Messerschmitt.

LOW PRIORITY

While Blohm & Voss wrestled with the intricacies of building the first BV 155 prototype, discussions were being held at the highest level about whether to cancel the type. The Entwicklungsbesprechung on March 17, 1944[7], reviewed the company's progress and the type's potential usefulness in the light of other developments.

A summary, under the heading 'Me 155', states: "It must be checked if the development of the Me 155 has to continue. Me 155 is an extreme high-altitude fighter with DB 603 + turbocharger TKL 15 being constructed by Dr Vogt (B&V). Schedule: First prototype with DB 603 but without TKL is expected in autumn 1944. The first versions of the turbine set may be available as specified in September 1944. However, an engine is not yet available."

Flugbaumeister Malz gave a brief presentation on the aircraft's expected performance with graphs: "The special high-altitude fighter has a maximum ceiling of over 16km. However, in terms of performance and strength, the aircraft is worthless below 12km. This working altitude (about 12km) is covered by the patterns Ta 152 H, Ta 154 (254), Do 335 (large wing area) and Ju 388.

"The working altitude of the Me 155 is only covered by the interceptors Me 163 and Me 262 with additional rocket boost which both, however, have low flight time at this altitude. Me 163 has 7.5 minutes at 16km and 8.5 minutes at 14km; it is not bad weather. Me 262 with rocket device has eight minutes' flight time at 16km and is operational in bad weather.

"Flugbaumeister Malz offered the following points as reasons not to drop the Me 155: 1) Uncertainty of the altitude performance of the jet engines.

2) The currently available interceptors are not reliable due to their low available attack time. The Me 155 should therefore not be abandoned before it can be assumed with some certainty that high-altitude performance can be achieved with the jet. Should the Me 155 be dropped, it should be ensured that the team of Dr Vogt does not fall apart."

Knemeyer, now promoted to oberstleutnant, told the meeting that "there are still considerable difficulties to be overcome in the extreme altitude zone in the case of both forms of propulsion. For the piston engine at such heights the issues of refrigerant, lubricant and fuel supply are still very unclear. The exhaust gas turbine will practically not be there before the spring of 1945. Since there are considerable issues to be resolved for both possibilities and the first (piston engine) brings no special advantage in terms of time, while the second (jet) under all circumstances must be ensured for the future, it is necessary to put all of our resources into the high-altitude jet engine.

"It is therefore proposed to stop the Me 155 project on the airframe side and to resume it in case of possibly negative results or time delays of the jet engine (TKL can be taken further on the Ju 488). The Me 155 can then be quickly revived. The current absence of a

ABOVE: Wooden mock-up of the BV 155 B's cockpit interior.

OPPOSITE: Three photographs of a model showing the final BV 155 B design from a Blohm & Voss report dated May 6, 1944.

ABOVE: Mock-up of the BV 155 B's forward fuselage. Getting the positioning of the aircraft's DB 603 U engine and its associated pipework exactly right was of critical importance.

ABOVE: Another view of the BV 155 B forward section mock-up.

management procedure must not be a reason for the Me 155 to continue, as this procedure must be developed with the utmost urgency".

Milch summarised: "If the enemy does not fly in squadron strength above 12km, the Me 155 is not required. If he appears at greater altitudes and the high-altitude jet fails, for the time being we have nothing between 13km and 15km. However, since it is unlikely that this combination would be correct and it makes no sense to create airframes without engines, the prototyping of the Me 155 can be stopped.

ABOVE: A third view of the BV 155 B mock-up.

"Cessation of the constructive development work is decisive. It is therefore for C-E to examine which work of Dr Vogt is still to be done in order to make the project so ready to move that it may be possible to continue it without the old B&V team elsewhere. A final decision will be taken after these investigations."

The outcome of this debate, while not a cancellation, appears to have been a downgrading of the BV 155's priority rating. As a result, it became more difficult for Blohm & Voss to acquire the materials, components and manpower necessary to progress the project.

A further construction meeting was held by the company on March 20[8] and the main topic for discussion was a recalculation of the V1's take-off weight up to 6250kg, compared to the previous total of 5600kg. This was due to the decision to fit armour plating in the cockpit, enlargement of the tailplane, excess weight in the structure and enlargement of equipment.

Thereafter, work on the BV 155 slowed considerably as Vogt's team turned their attention to completing the first BV 40 prototypes. At a GL-Besprechung on April 7[9], BMW director Walter Schilo referred several times to the BV 155 with its exhaust gas turbine as a "special solution" and reported that Daimler-Benz was well advanced with its DB 603 engine. He said: "The last word has not yet been spoken about the BV 155."

The definitive design of the BV 155 B-1 was embodied in drawing 8-155.00-12 on April 19, 1944[10]. This had a wing area of 39m², a wingspan of 20.25m and a length of 12.5m. A joint BV 155 and BV 40 construction meeting on April 24[11] heard the results of ongoing work at Rechlin, with a decision to alter the number of fuel tanks in the aircraft to four – a change which would not be made in the BV 155 V1. In addition, Junkers was to carry out design work on a fire extinguishing system for the wings and engine bay.

A further GL-Besprechung on April 28[12] heard from Professor Günther Bock of the Forschungsführung des Reichsluftfahrtministers und Oberbefehlshabers der Luftwaffe at Göttingen – the Luftwaffe's aviation research command, known as 'FoFü' for short – that the 36% aluminium and 64% cheap steel material composition of the BV 155 made it an interesting development which saved on scarce aluminium. Nevertheless, work on the

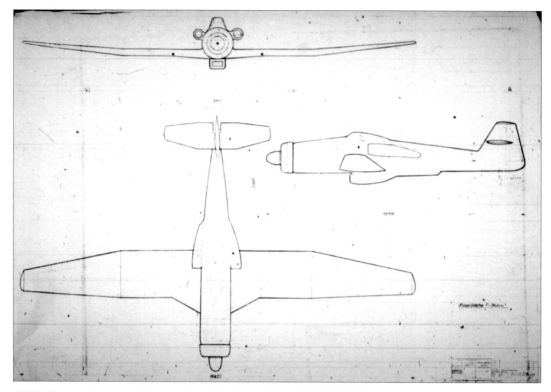

ABOVE: The only known surviving drawing of the Blohm & Voss P 205.01-01. The design had a wingspan of 18.65m and was 12.1m long. Its most notable feature, however, was its twin intake scoops extending from the fuselage sides. This arrangement was dropped in favour of what became the BV 155 C.

aircraft at Blohm & Voss during May and June consisted of little more than carrying out a series of strength calculations and wind tunnel tests based on the 8-155.00-12 design and corresponding with various companies concerning components.

The Rechlin weekly report for the period from June 11 to June 17, 1944[13], noted: "BV 155 is still running under completely insufficient urgency rating 'SS'. Daimler-Benz has still not delivered engine mock-up. Latest commitment is to deliver at the end of July. Due to this delaying tactic, a corresponding delay in delivery is to be expected."

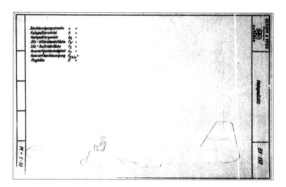

ABOVE: This poor quality drawing from circa August 1944 shows the basic operation of an ejection seat in the BV 155 B. Neither of the two B-series prototypes would end up being fitted with one, however.

On July 1 Rechlin wrote to Heinkel[14] asking for details of the ejection seat fitted to its He 219 with reference to the possibility of using the same design in the BV 155.

REVIVAL AND REDESIGN

The Rechlin weekly report for the period from July 2 to July 8, 1944[15], noted with apparent exasperation: "According to the current situation of prototyping at B&V, it may not even be possible to build the V1 of the BV 155, let alone the five commissioned prototypes. If this development really does matter in any way, it is necessary to immediately remove the current urgency level 'SS' and classify the entire development with an urgency to procure both people and material. Consideration must be given to the further development of the aircraft model in order to expand the contract into a larger number of other prototypes after examination."

Reichsmarschall Hermann Göring made a presentation to Adolf Hitler on July 8, 1944, outlining a new programme of development and production for the remainder of 1944 and 1945 which recommended the discontinuation of various types to concentrate primarily on fighters. In particular, production of the Me 410 was to be stopped immediately and production of the He 177 to be scaled back.

The deputy of war production minister Albert Speer, Karl-Otto Saur, outlined the consequences arising from Hitler's approval of this programme at a meeting of the Jägerstab on July 9[16]. The sixth point stated that Diesing, now a full Oberst, "while maintaining his capacity as Chief of the Luftwaffe Planning Office, was also charged with the deputy management of the GL/C Technical Office". And the 10th point stated that Diesing's first job in this role was "development BV 155: emergency assessment". However, this does not appear to have happened immediately.

Blohm & Voss met representatives of Daimler-Benz on July 12-13 to discuss progress on the DB 603 U and according to Daimler-Benz's post-meeting report[17]: "The purpose of the meeting was to clarify all pending questions regarding the power plant and engine DB 603 U for the BV 155 with TKL 15." It was noted that of the five prototypes planned, the V1 to V4 would be the 'first version' while the V5 would be the 'second version'. Evidently, "B&V

ABOVE: The partially constructed fuselage of the BV 155 B V1.

is currently developing the BV 155 with regard to the radiator arrangement. Instead of the previous arrangement, here a radiator is planned as an installation in front of the engine. After reviewing the sketches by B&V, DB proposed on the basis of new project documents to accept small necessary changes to the DB project and to use the cooling unit of DB for the BV 155 second version".

With the BV 155 B-1 on go-slow, Blohm & Voss had evidently been given time to rethink the aircraft's radiator arrangement and come up with a better one – repositioning the radiator in front of the engine.

According to the Rechlin weekly report for July 9 to July 15, 1944[18]: "BV 155 mock-up final inspection took place. E-Stelle has until today received no testing order with number and urgency. The number of people busy with the prototype is far below the number planned, so that a timely completion of the prototype is not to be expected. Urgency is still 'SS'.

"It is necessary to carry out a precise schedule for the prototype construction with appropriate provision of the required workers. At the same time C-E 3 is to request a corresponding flow of TKL 15 exhaust turbines in order to have them in good time for the necessary further development BV 155 (larger number of prototypes absolutely necessary)

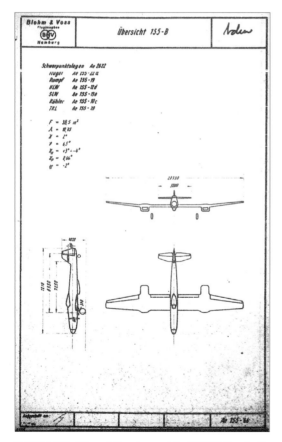 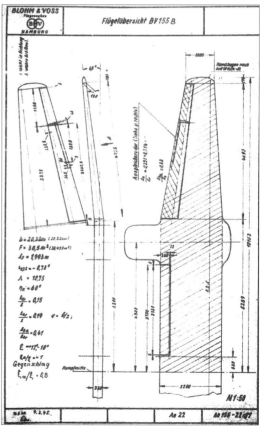

ABOVE LEFT: Although the shape of the BV 155 B as built was very similar to the 8-155.00-12 drawing of April 1944, its dimensions did vary slightly as the realities of building it became clear. This drawing from circa August 1944 gives a wingspan of 20.33m compared to 20.25m in 8-155.00-12. ABOVE RIGHT: Drawing of the BV 155 B's wing with two dates – August 16, 1944, and February 9, 1945.

and for a possible series start. The same is to be done in the field of engines and radiators. The required number of aircraft and the start of production must be announced in good time to B&V."

The report for the following week[19] stated: "Urgency of fighter BV 155 still unclear. At development meeting on July 26, BV 155 must be required with the highest possible pressure."

A Blohm & Voss report of July 25[20] compared the expected performance of the drawing 8-155.00-12 version of the BV 155 with that of a new design – the P 205.01-01. This aircraft had a conventional annular radiator in front of its engine plus intakes on either side of the fuselage behind the cockpit. The starboard intake fed the turbosupercharger while air from the port intake was passed through a heat exchanger. After being compressed in the engine supercharger, the intake air was directed to an after-cooler in a large duct beneath the fuselage before passing to the inlet manifold. Exhaust from the supercharger turbine was discharged downwards and rearwards beneath the fuselage. All of this allowed a wingspan reduction to 18.65m and a length reduction to 12.1m.

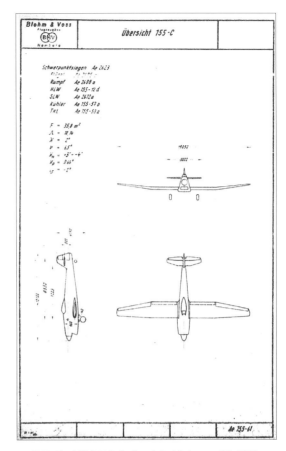

ABOVE: The BV 155 C design dated February 22, 1945. This very basic drawing is the only known three-view of the type.

The introduction to the report states: "The following pages contain the flight performance for BV 155 as of July 1944. The performance data according to the specifications of January 1944 changed only marginally thereafter. Added to this are the P 205 performance figures as a further development of the BV 155."

Take-off weight for both designs was given as 6000kg but "it should be noted, however, that the P 205 is lighter than the BV 155 with the same fuel load – 200kg". And both had a 3.7m diameter propeller. Performance of the P 205 was expected to marginally exceed that of the BV 155 B but it appears that the company ultimately decided not to pursue this radiator arrangement any further.

The development meeting on July 26, 1944, was pivotal. The number of BV 155 prototypes on order was increased to seven and it would appear that the type's urgency level was also raised. As a result, Blohm & Voss began to rapidly pick up the pace.

The company draw up a chart on July 27[21] showing how each of the seven prototypes would be built and what it would be used to test. Now only the V1-V3 would be built as BV 155 B-1s, with V4-V7 being a new version – the BV 155 C. This design had just one large intake under its nose to supply all of its cool air requirements. The 'C' had a wingspan of 19.05m, a wing area of 30.5m² and like the P 205 it was 12.1m long.

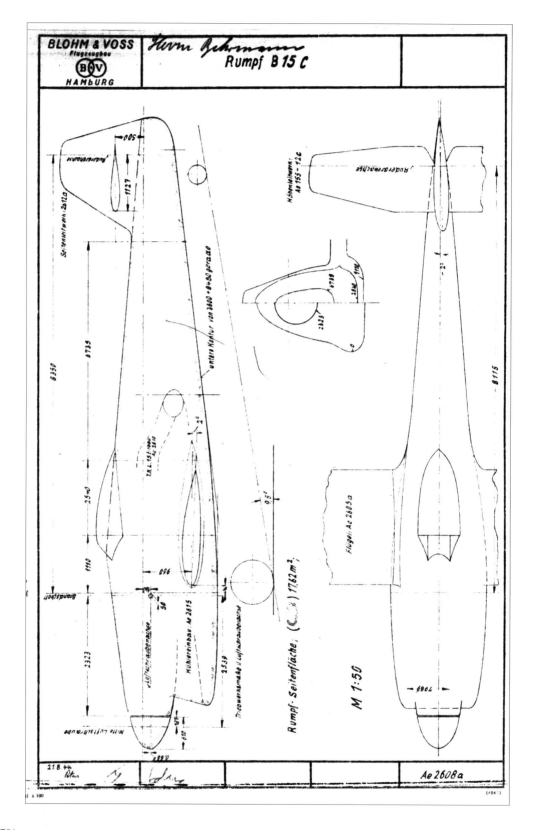

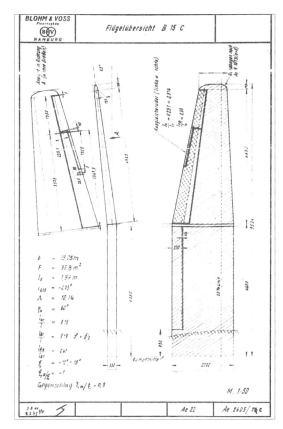

ABOVE: The BV 155 C's wing form was similar to that of the BV 155 B but considerably simplified thanks to the removal of the wing-mounted radiators. This drawing has two dates on it – August 3, 1944, and February 9, 1945.

OPPOSITE: A side-view drawing of the BV 155 C's fuselage dated August 21, 1944.

The V1-V3 were to be built without weapons while the V4-V7 would all be fully armed. Construction of the BV 155 B V1 was to be completed in December 1944 and its purpose was engine testing. The V2 and V3 would be completed in January and February 1945 respectively and would both be used for general flight testing. The BV 155 C V4, for flight mechanics testing, would be ready in April 1945, while the V5, ready in May, would be fitted with an ejection seat. Both the V6 and V7 would be ready in June 1945 and both would be fitted with the Junkers wing fire extinguishing system.

Heinkel sent Blohm & Voss a bundle of documents relating to the ejection seat of its He 219 night fighter on July 31 and these were duly assessed with the aid of personnel from Rechlin[22].

ENGINE INSTALLATION

On August 2 it was calculated that the take-off weight of the BV 155 C was 6400kg with a normal load or 7000kg in overload and work on designing the BV 155 C's radiator arrangement continued[23]. There was a meeting at Rechlin on August 19 to discuss equipping the BV 155 V2 and V3 with cameras and other sensors to record test data such as fuel tank pressure, turbocharger lubricant outlet temperature, turbocharger air temperature, temperature of the 3000W generator, temperature of the exhaust pipe trough and air temperature within the engine compartment. The V3 would get additional sensors to measure air temperature before and after the heat exchanger, turbocharger speed, exhaust pressure and positioning of the exhaust flaps.

Ten days later there was another meeting at Rechlin[24], this time to discuss the ejection seat installation for the BV 155 V5. It was decided that Dornier should send B&V a complete example of its Do 335 ejection seat including all controls and ancillary equipment. But "because the seat can not be easily installed because of the large seat pan, it should be converted to a normal parachute with dimensions 380 x 330 (width times depth in flight direction). For the BV 155 the seat parachute 550 is recommended. This parachute is usable up to 550km/h, has the above dimensions and is built by the companies Autoflug and Schröder, both in Berlin".

The Dornier seat was apparently better than the Heinkel model because with a longer acceleration path "an ejection speed of 17m/sec is achieved (compared to 13.5m/sec in

Heinkel). This is very favourable, because according to Dr Irrgang calculated trajectory against the shot attempts from the He 219 in flight proved to be too low".

A meeting was held with representatives of the AVA on September 12 at Finkenwärder[25] to discuss ongoing developments with the BV 155 C's cooling system. At the outset it was stated that the radiator arrangement planned for the C-series "represents a favourable solution" but there were concerns about Hirth's capability to manufacture the necessary type 2279 turbochargers. It was proposed that the more easily built 2426 turbo should be examined even though "the installation of this turbine means a loss in peak altitude of at least 2km, so that the task underlying the whole project would no longer be fulfilled".

It was suggested that B&V should switch radiator suppliers from SKF to Fimag because the Fimag product offered ongoing development and improved heat removal. Finally, it was noted that engine manufacturers would henceforth be required to use steel to the greatest extent possible and with the BV 155 C the engine cowling would also have to be made from steel.

The following day Blohm & Voss received a communication from E-Stelle Travemünde[26] concerning the BV 155's camouflage which read: "The BV 155 shall have on the upper surface the colours 81 olive brown and 82 light green. The mottling spacing and placement should be similar to the BV [Bf] 109's camouflage scheme. The fuselage sides, side of the vertical tailplane and leading edge of the wing and horizontal stabiliser should be painted colour tone 76. Hereafter, except for the wing and horizontal stabiliser's leading edge, the aircraft should then be in a cloudy overspray with colour tones 81 + 82.

"Also, looking ahead there will be a simplification of paint schemes which we should know shortly and will publish. Afterwards, for the above mentioned aircraft, which will be used for day service, camouflage on the underside should be deleted. With the mottle scheme, it should be applied on the aircraft sheet metal between camouflage and its painted line. The pattern is to be soft flowing lines. The colour scheme is to be sprayed on at the present time.

"In case of needed puttying (aircraft putty 7270.99), it should be applied on bare metal beyond the border lines of the paint scheme and the bare metal should be polished in the usual way but no camouflage on top of the putty. The painting of the undersurface is being deleted to economise."

On September 15, 1944, a telegram[27] was sent out to all Luftwaffe commands stating that: "The Herr Reichsmarschall [Göring] has banned the designation 'Höhenjäger'; it is to be replaced by the word 'Begleitjäger' [escort fighter]." The purpose of this redesignation is unclear but it did result in the BV 155 being referred to as the 'Begleitsjägers 8-155 mit DB 603 U und Turbolader 9-2279' in later reports.

The ejection seat was again discussed on September 25[28] and it was noted that the Dornier system would indeed be installed in the BV 155 V5 even though the seat, designed for a special 380 x 380mm parachute pack, would have to be modified to suit the standard 380 x 330mm pack. The rear wall of the pressure cabin would also need to be modified to accommodate the bulk of the ejection seat's compressed air cylinder. In addition: "The upper edge of the pressurised cabin is so narrow that the armrests of the seat do not go through. However, it will make little difference to the pilot if the armrests are brought together to the required extent. It is important to ensure that the control box is placed directly in front of the right armrest."

Preparations to receive the BV 155 V1's engine were made on the same day[29] and it would seem that the first three DB 603 Us were delivered over the next four days. On September 28

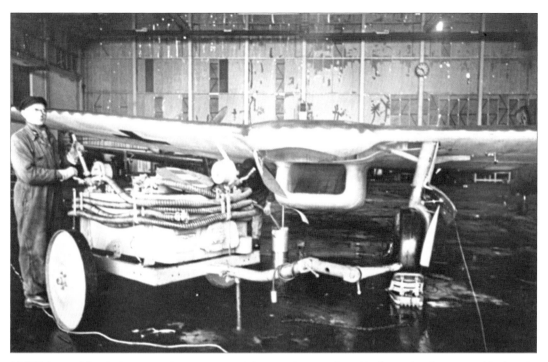

ABOVE: A technician drains coolant from the BV 155 B V1's starboard radiator. The innovative diagonal positioning of the radiator within the nacelle is clearly visible.

ABOVE: The engine bay of the BV 155 B V1. The prominent engine bearer arm is visible along with the corresponding bulge it necessitated in the cowling panel above it.

28 it was noted that parts and spares for all three of the first three prototypes were now being received and logged within the company's main parts supply[30].

An inspection of the BV 155 B engine installation mock-up took place on September 29[31]. Firstly, it was noted that the engines supplied for the BV 155 B had been delivered with a reduction gear ratio of 1:1.93, but this reduced propeller efficiency by 1-2% so engines for the BV 155 C would need to have a ratio of 1:2.07 instead. Furthermore, Daimler-Benz had supplied VDM 13009 gearboxes but according to the mock-up inspection report "VDM needs to clarify if this gear is sufficient for the four-blade propeller. If this is not the case, then the 13030 must be delivered for the V1-V3 engines, otherwise the testing of the entire system and the aircraft cannot take place at all.

"The installation of the gearbox 13030, intended for the BV 155 C engines, already means a conversion of the gear housing and thus a change (reduction) of the lubricant reservoir. Further changes are to be feared, since according to the latest communication from DB for the engine also the Me P 8 propeller is to be used". The P 8 was a reversible pitch propeller designed and built by Messerschmitt.

The mock-up report also noted that Daimler-Benz and Heinkel-Hirth needed to determine what the usefulness of methanol injection would be but further noted that the installation of the turbocharger was fine. Verification of the radiator fittings had been carried out on a model aircraft and it was decided that the BV 155 B's heat exchanger could probably be carried over to the BV 155 C pending the outcome of further tests.

There was some concern that both the upper and lower engine cowlings might come loose at high speed, so two additional attachment points would be added for each. And adopting the Daimler-Benz engine frame, it was noted, would result in "a pronounced bulge" in the upper engine cowl. B&V was to clarify whether this frame would still be supplied by Daimler-Benz and if not a new frame would need to be designed – which would eliminate the bulges.

FINAL ADJUSTMENTS

A Blohm & Voss planning chart of October 10, 1944[32], shows that three BV 155 Bs were now on order plus 27 BV 155 Cs. It was expected that a single BV 155 B would be completed in December 1944, another in January 1945 and the third in February. The completion of the first BV 155 C was due in March, two more were to follow in April and three more in May. Four would be finished in June, five in July and six each in August and September.

While these plans were being drawn up, Blohm & Voss's construction office worked on routing 0.0453 cubic metres of warm air per second from the turbocharger system to heat the weapons and ammunition of the BV 155 C via a 55mm/40mm pipe. On October 12 it was noted that the company had received data suggesting that outside temperatures at an altitude of 16km could fluctuate between –39°C in the summer and –72°C during the winter, while the temperature of the piped air would be 50°C at ground level and 117°C at 16km. A valve in the hot air duct would enable the system to be disabled during the summer[33].

On November 4, as work on the BV 155 V1 neared its conclusion, a programme of tests for the aircraft's first flight was drawn up by the company's department of flight mechanics[34] and further minor tweaks were made, including adjustments to the Focke-Wulf-sourced tailwheel lock – the bolts for which kept "jumping out". Tests were also carried out on the pressure cabin, based on a Henschel design, to ensure tightness.

Meanwhile, the organisation of Germany's aircraft design and development structure had changed again with the formation of the new Entwicklungshauptkommission (EHK), chaired by Roluf Lucht, on September 15, 1944, and on November 8 Vogt responded to an EHK memo which posed the question 'Why produce the Otto [Otto being a contemporary German nickname for piston engines, after the man regarded as their inventor – Nikolaus Otto] fighter?'[35]

The memo had asked the major aircraft manufacturers, the leaders of whom were all members of the EHK, to consider whether production of aircraft such as the Bf 109 and Fw 190 should be transitioned as soon as possible to the production of the Me 262, He 162, Ar 234 and their successors.

Vogt replied by discussing both piston engine and jet engine projects being worked on by his staff – specifically the DB 603-engined pusher-prop P 208.03, the HeS 011 jet-propelled P 209.02, the company's failed contender for the Volksjäger competition, the P 211.01, and also "the operational efficiency of the extreme high-altitude fighter BV 155 is referred to on several occasions, in order to indicate its technical possibilities which go far beyond the scope of this investigation".

Under 'climbing power', Vogt wrote: "The Volksjäger has the lowest climbing speed and lowest ceiling. Their ceiling being equal, the climbing speed of the Otto fighter is, above an altitude of 2000m, higher than that of the high-speed fighter. At its full pressure altitude, around about 9km, its climbing power is 50% higher than that of the jet fighter. The high-altitude fighter BV 155 outstrips the Volksjäger above an altitude of 8km and the two others above 12km." He concluded that, on balance, both piston engine and jet aircraft had their uses depending on what roles needed to be filled.

ABOVE: Opening a single large panel on the side of the BV 155 B allowed excellent access to the supercharger compartment. To the left is the pressurised battery container, above that is the glycol coolant tank, and in the centre is the intercooler. The white cylinder on the right is the turbine lubricant container and below it is the fire extinguisher. Below the fuselage, the ventral cover has been left off to display the main air intake duct and turbine blade air duct.

ABOVE: The interior of the BV 155 B V1's cockpit while still being pieced together.

According to the minutes of a meeting held (probably by the EHK) on November 21-22, referenced in postwar British report German Aircraft: New and Projected Types[36]: "The development of BV 155 high-altitude fighters for operation up to 16km was considered imperative, although at the time of the meeting only a small experimental series had been ordered."

Work in December included preparing the pitot tube and resolving issues with the various measuring systems installed on the V1 – including the installation of a switch to activate two cameras. On December 6, the RLM wrote to E-Stelle Tarnewitz regarding the development and testing of weaponry for the BV 155[37]. Armament was to be an MK 108 mounted in the aircraft's DB 603 with 70 rounds of ammunition and two MG 151/20s in the wings with 200 rounds each. For the gunsight, "the installation of the EZ 42 has to be investigated and pattern installation carried out for a later conversion of the series 8-155 from Revi 16 B to EZ 42. Changeover date depends on the possibility of procurement". It was noted that the allocation of a single EZ 42 sight for installation in the BV 155 had been initiated.

Representatives of E-Stelle Rechlin visited Finkenwärder on December 9 to examine the pressure cabin installation and made several recommendations including a provision for opening the cockpit canopy from the outside. Stiffness in the rudder controls was resolved and the Deutsche Versuchsanstalt für Luftfahrt (DVL) was consulted for advice on investigating flutter on the BV 155 B.

Static vibration tests were carried out on the V1 beginning on January 3[38] – for which a number of components had to be removed – and a team from Rechlin carried out a two-day combined inspection of the BV 155 C mock-up and BV 155 B V1 on January 15-16, 1945[39].

A whole host of observations were made concerning the mock-up and changes were required in the resulting report, including switching the exhaust steam outlet from the left side to the right side of the engine; using direct oil cooling instead of secondary circuit cooling; the bespoke B&V oil and fuel cap lock was to be swapped for that of the Heinkel He 162, since the two were of similar design; MW 50 injection would be a feature of the BV 155 C (B&V "drawing attention to the fact that the radiator as designed would not be sufficient for MW 50 operation on hot summer days"); head armour could be retrofitted for the pilot later; B&V was reminded that all steel and iron parts in the area of the cockpit compass needed to be demagnetised; and accessibility of components was generally fine as was the layout of the cockpit instruments.

It was noted that the BV 155 C would be equipped with FuG 15 radio and FuG 25 identification transponder, with the antenna for the former strung between the fuselage and the rudder and the antenna for the latter under the fuselage. Armament was an MK 108 motor cannon with 75 rounds "accessible through a hatch from the pilot's compartment", which was fine. In each wing was an MG 151/20 with 100 rounds but the locks holding the ammunition boxes in place did not seem sufficient to the inspectors.

The gunsight installed was a Revi 16 B, although it was expected that this would be upgraded to an Askania EZ-42 Adler sight. The E-Stelle was to "clarify immediately whether installing the Adler with ZFR-3 [telescopic sight] in conjunction with

ABOVE: The BV 155 B V1's undercarriage under construction. During the aircraft's few test flights it was found that the wheels tended to throw mud and debris up into the radiator nacelles during take-offs and landings.

ABOVE: Close up of the BV 155 B V1's undercarriage.

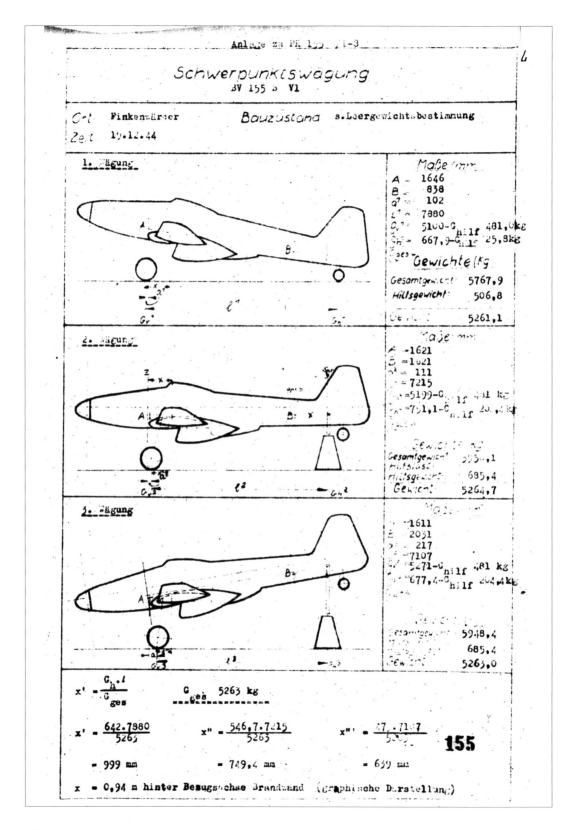

MK 103 is still interesting". The mock-up was also fitted with an Rb 75/30 camera in the fuselage for reconnaissance, with a side hatch provided for changing the film. It was proposed that a second Rb 75/30 could be fitted in tandem "for better space utilisation", the two cameras being pivoted 9° to the right and left respectively and fitted with an interval timer so that both would take photographs at exactly the same time.

Blohm & Voss engineer Schukat and RLM staff engineer Gessner met on January 22, 1945, to discuss new armaments available to be considered for Blohm & Voss's P 212 single jet fighter project[40]; it was mentioned that the P 212 could make use of the EZ 42 gunsight and it was noted that a single example of this device was already available at Blohm & Voss for installation in the BV 155.

A report on the heaviness of the BV 155 B V1's controls was produced on January 24[41], which found that they were generally much heavier than those measured on a Bf 109 G-1, Werk-Nr. 14002. And on January 30, a list of final checks was drawn up for the measuring and test equipment fitted to the BV 155 V1 ahead of its first flight, which was expected to be imminent[42].

January 31 saw cracks appearing in the overall system of aircraft development and production with Hitler's announcement of a new Führer-Notprogramm or 'Leader Emergency Programme' for aircraft[43]. The number of aircraft types in production was to be reduced still further to just a handful – although exactly which types this encompassed had not been decided. It was unclear what would happen to aircraft which had not yet entered full series production. ●

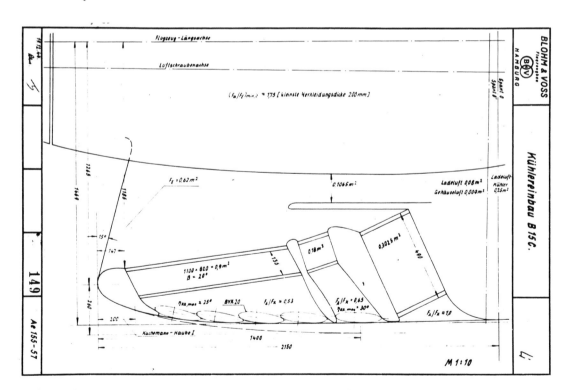

ABOVE: Blohm & Voss drawing showing a side view of the BV 155 C's chin radiator dated December 19, 1944.

OPPOSITE: A report on tests to determine the BV 155 B V1's centre of gravity, also dated December 19, 1944.

Chapter 6
The beginning and the end
February to May 1945
(Flight tests and capture)

ABOVE: One of the few known photos showing the completed BV 155 B V1.

A list of 232 minor defects identified on the BV 155 V1 was reported on February 1, 1945[1], following a factory quality control inspection. This included everything from two rivets missing from the top of the inner aileron to the hand crank for sliding the cockpit canopy into place being loose. While these were being corrected, tests were carried out with a mock-up of the BV 155 B's cockpit canopy, using plywood panels instead of Plexiglas, to determine whether the Fw 190-style emergency ejection system would function correctly. This concluded that there was so much surplus energy in the system that "a perfect functioning of the launching device can be expected even with a glazed roof".

BV 155 V1 was handed over to Blohm & Voss's flight section on February 5[2]. The handover report noted that the aircraft's serial number was Werk-Nr. 360051 and that all defects identified by the factory had been resolved, insofar as they affected flight safety. An undercarriage test had taken place but a further check of the hydraulic function would need to be made with the engine running before the first flight and the same applied to the aileron locking mechanism.

The switch for the electric locking cylinder of the left aileron was not working and could not be repaired at that time, "firstly, because no spare part is available and secondly, no access cover is provided". As a result, the left cylinder was now controlled from the right side switch. "This complaint must of course be resolved as soon as possible". The engine had been set up by the Daimler-Benz engineer and its automatic adjustment would be tested before take-off. However, the generator's insulation was found to be inadequate and if this could not be improved it would have to be replaced. A new one had already been ordered.

The cables connecting the inner ailerons had not been extended but it was noted that clearances were very tight and that correcting this issue would only be possible via a major rebuild. In fact, the entire control system suffered from excess friction, which had been reported. The fire extinguisher system had not been cleared for operation and the pressure cabin had not been pressure tested, nor was the canopy airtight.

The first flight test of Werk-Nr. 360051 took place three days later on February 8, 1945, with Blohm & Voss chief test pilot Helmut 'Wasa' Rodig at the controls. His report[3] notes that the aircraft's take-off weight was 5910kg and the centre of gravity was set at 28%.

He then states: "Roll: On starting up rotation cannot be stopped, even with full application of the rudder and brakes. The lack of sufficient centring is instrumental in this behaviour. The brakes are not enough.

"Start: In the start (without flaps), the aircraft was on slow throttle (wind 6m/sec) to keep well on course. There was no significant load change during or after taking off. Short rolling distance.

"Flight: Immediately after the start a strong flow of coolant was visible behind the main radiator (starboard). After reaching 200m height, the engine was throttled heavily (0.8 atmospheres boost pressure). As a result, the outflow of coolant was greatly reduced and the decision was then made to try a normal landing on the airfield. The temperature of the coolant rose slowly and had just passed 100°C when approaching the runway.

"An assessment of the flight characteristics, even only a rough one, cannot be given under these circumstances. Rudder and aileron forces were perceived as low, though noticeably higher from the rudder. Aileron effectiveness appears deficient, especially at low speeds (landing).

"Landing: Approach and landing were considerably hampered by the glaring absence of the airspeed indicator (device connected incorrectly). Instinctively minimum speed was flown, since a go-around would have resulted in the certain destruction of the engine. Altitude reserves were used to slip onto the edge of the strip. Landing was one-sided on the right wheel without strong impact. Roll-out distance low."

He listed seven complaints about the aircraft: airspeed indicator unclear; rudder pedal support too soft allowing the pedal to rest on top of the coolant pipe; brake pedals out of reach when rudder pedals fully applied, seat padding would push the pilot forward a few centimetres; with the pilot strapped in, the mechanism for ejecting the canopy was triggered by the straps ("the system must be better protected against unwanted activity"); the brakes were inadequate; strong interference on the FuG 16 making it impossible to use during flight, and the cause of the coolant leak was two brackets slipping off a tube above the radiator.

Rodig noted that the same thing had happened a few days earlier during an engine test. He wrote: "In order to avoid disturbances of this kind, which can very quickly lead to damage or loss of the aircraft by means of an emergency landing, in further testing, a thorough remedy must be provided here. The provision of the pipes with a second flange and greater overlap of the sleeves appears promising. In its present condition, it is not possible to carry out further testing.

"It is intended, after provisional remedy, to carry out a few flights in order to obtain a rough impression of the characteristics of the aircraft. It is proposed to use the time necessary for the change of the coolant pipelines, to install the measuring system, leak test the cockpit and do all the other outstanding work."

The following day it was noted that the BV 155 V3 had been cancelled and "the BV 155 V4 is now being equipped as a test aircraft for the flight vibration tests[4]. The conversion of the cockpit and the canopy as well as the installation of the ejection seat follows drawing 100 Sk 155.229. The TKL is not installed. Further details are still to be determined".

SECOND FLIGHT

And the day after that, February 10, 1945, the second flight test of the V1 took place with Rodig as pilot again. Take-off weight was 10kg lighter at 5900kg and centre of gravity was the same.

Rodig wrote[5]: "Start: In the softened airfield grassy area there were disturbing influences on the wide track undercarriage. Despite the wheel sinking on one side, the aircraft took off start a short start. Fast course correction was hampered by the great friction of the rudder. Start otherwise without complaints.

"Flight: Undercarriage pulled in for the first time. Retracting time (16 sec.) is considered too long. Undercarriage reset on single actuation. Experimentally installed display for closing the landing gear flaps does not work despite repeated actuation of the landing gear switch. After the flight, dents were seen in the rear left flap which indicate that the flaps do not close properly. Due to low clouds, speed of 350km/h was not exceeded. Aircraft is in equilibrium at this speed with almost top-heavy tailplane. For higher speed, trim will not be sufficient without changing the tailpane edge trim.

"Initiation of a rougher stability test at 320km/h shows lack of longitudinal stability. How far this is influenced by large rudder friction remains to be determined. Further flight tests had to be stopped as the oil temperature rose above the maximum limit. Undercarriage extended freely at above 250km/h .

"Landing: Approach with 170km/h. The view of the runway is bad. Touchdown is very soft. Pulling of the control stick is hampered by parachute and straps."

Rodig had six complaints this time: the back cushion now included still wasn't enough for his size, which he gives as 174cm (5ft 8½in); the cause of the high oil temperatures needed to be determined but was probably due to poor ventilation of the cooling system ("deficiencies of this kind are continuously raised by the company and the DB mechanic"); the undercarriage doors were not closing properly, resulting in the left flap being dented; the undercarriage struts were very springy; the brakes were better but still not good enough and actuation of the cooling control was difficult.

The war diary of Ulrich Diesing (who had been appointed head of the Technischen Luftwaffenrüstung (air technical equipment) on August 1, 1944) for the week from February 5 to 11[6], states: "BV 155. The first 2 flights without significant events or results."

For the same week he wrote of "complete confusion" where the Führer-Notprogramm was concerned. Nobody knew where the axe would fall. And although the EHK had announced an 'Entwicklungs-Notprogramm' for aircraft development projects, Diesing wrote that Speer and Saur did not consider this necessary.

On February 14, B&V proposed to E-Stelle Rechlin[7] that an air duct should be installed in the cockpit canopy of the BV 155 C but the test centre responded the following day to say that this might result in a deterioration of pilot visibility – instead it was proposed that a pipe should be installed which would do the same job of allowing air to enter the cockpit.

Evidently the measuring system had finally been fitted to the V1 by February 19 because a set of instructions for its operation was issued[8]. The cameras could take a total of 40 shots and one needed to be taken before take-off. Two days later, further vibration tests were carried out on the V1 with the movements of the oil filter against a fixed point being measuring when the engine was started. Movements recorded were within the maximum 10mm allowable. Engine stall vibration tests were then undertaken.

THIRD FLIGHT

Rodig once again took the BV 155 V1 up on February 28, 1945. The take-off weight and centre of gravity were unchanged and his flight report afterwards[9] said: "Start: Despite very soft airfield the start went perfectly. Slight tendency to break, caused by sinking on one side (wide track), could be corrected. Low rolling distance.

ABOVE and BELOW: Two further views of the BV 155 B V1 before it was wrecked in a crash landing on April 23, 1945, with Luftwaffe pilot Kurt Reuth at the controls.

ABOVE: The partially assembled BV 155 B V2 as the American CIOS team found it in June 1945.

ABOVE: Another view of the BV 155 B V2 – showing that the tailfin and tailplanes were attached before British troops entered Hamburg in May 1945.

"Flight: Retracting the undercarriage took moderately longer than during the second flight. Engaging took place only after pressing the switch twice. Display for landing gear doors did not come on and there were similar dents on the left flap as on the previous flight. The coolant temperature display (circuit I) was already reading 107-110°C at the start and remained the same during the rest of the flight (still allowable). The operation of the cooling flaps of circuit I was so difficult that an adjustment of the thermostat was not possible on 'open', even with the greatest possible effort.

"In order to ensure the tightness of the pipes, the flight was not extended. Once the measuring system (photo and writing instruments) were switched on, the landing gear was extended. Even when extending it took longer for the gear to engage despite twice pressing the emergency switch.

"Landing: Fully braced and very soft. Nevertheless, very deep springing of the struts. When landing, as well as at the start on the muddy airfield, occurs very heavy polluting of the radiators with dirt thrown up by the undercarriage wheels.

"After checking the coolant system, it was hoped that another start could be made afterwards. However, it turned out that the rudder had become very difficult again and subsequently a number of further problems emerged."

Again Rodig complained about the rudder pedals resting on the coolant pipes, making the rudder controls very heavy and endangering the pipes. He mentioned the difficulties he had encountered in adjusting the thermostat and said it had been discovered that oil had been getting into the air mixture before it reached the engine. This was being caused by oil escaping from the vent valve of the turbine's oil tank and dripping into the intake shaft. The wheel doors on the left side were closing early, jamming the landing gear. While this was being inspected, a crack in the steel wing spar box was discovered. Finally, switching on the measuring equipment caused strong interference on the radio, which made communication with the ground impossible.

In early March, a chart was issued showing all the developments included in the EHK's Entwicklung-Notprogramm[10]. This included the BV 155 alongside the night fighter Me 262, variants of the Fw 190 and Ta 152, He 162 with Jumo 004 and He 162 S trainer, Ar 234 with HeS 011, the 1-TL-Jäger day fighter competition, the 2-TL-Jäger night and bad weather fighter competition, Grossbomber competition, DFS 346 high-speed research aircraft, Hs 132 and EF 126 ground-attack aircraft, Natter rocket-propelled interceptor, Fi 103 with 005 Porsche engine and various other missiles.

On March 7, a Blohm & Voss memo was issued regarding flight hours "for urgent pilot projects"[11]. During March the BV 155 V1 would be required to fly for 10 hours and 15 in April, the memo stating "These flight hours are required for the testing of the new engine (DB 603 U with turbocharger 2279) and the high-altitude cabin (welded steel construction). The working altitude of the aircraft is 14 to 16km."

The BV 155 V2 was to fly for 10 hours in April and "the flight measurements carried out with the BV 155 V2 are intended as a completion of the measurements on BV 155 V1". In addition, a Bf 109 G "with split rudder" was to fly four hours in March and six in April. "The flights provided with this aircraft serve to improve the currently very objectionable flight behaviour in the attack run. At the same time the flights are to serve as a test of the targeting for BV 155 C."

Five days after that, on March 12, Dr Vogt wrote to Willy Messerschmitt outlining the state of BV 155 development[12]. He wrote: "You will receive enclosed the desired documents. 8-155 B: In taking over the task from your company, we kept to the original plans to accommodate the extensive radiators in the wings.

"8-155 C: When the construction was almost finished and assembly [of the BV 155 B V1] had begun, further considerations resulted in a substantial increase in demand on the entire cooling system, i.e. engine water, engine oil and turbocharger with two stages. However, this could only happen after we found a satisfactory solution for the fuselage installation of very large radiator surfaces.

"The Technical Office shared our view all the more as it helped to remedy the precarious state of the coolant cycle with regard to its large internal circulation resistances. The result was the C series, which is intended as the starting point for the series production.

"Given the advanced state of the B, this was not stopped and continued in two airframes because it will bring a worthwhile use for the flight testing of the TK 15 exhaust gas storage set.

"The completion dates are as follows: 155 B V1: now in flight testing. V2: mid-April ready to fly. V3: stopped. 155 C V4: Mid-May ready to fly. V5: mid-June ready to fly." He then indicated that dates had not yet been determined for the 27 C-series aircraft that were on order – V6-V30 – but "given the current state of developments in relation to the urgency of the Führer-Notprogramm, we are unable to provide reliable information on the course of the V series".

At the FoFü, Professor Bock wrote a letter on March 12, 1945, giving the state of the Notprogramm[13], which had already been pared back from 10 aircraft – the Ju 88, Bf 109, Ta 152, He 162, Fw 190, Ar 234, Me 262, Do 335, Ar 396 and Mistel combinations – to just six: Ju 88, Ta 152/190, He 162, Ar 234, Me 262 and Ar 396. The BV 155 was not included and neither were the Bf 109 and Do 335.

For the period of March 5 to 15, Diesing wrote in his diary[14]: "8-155 not yet included in the emergency programme. There are already 35 men removed from the prototype work. B&V has received from EHK in consultation with FL-E a telex, which has said it has been requested for inclusion in the emergency programme (6 aircraft)."

Another flight testing programme was drawn up for the BV 155 on March 20[15] which said: "On the next flights of the BV 155 V1 the following must be considered by the pilot: 1) In order to obtain a clear picture of the behaviour of the loading pressure and temperatures on the aircraft, climbing flights with maximum climb and combat performance (100%) are to be carried out. 2) During the ascent, the aircraft pilot must take a picture at the most regular time intervals (about 1 minute).

"3) If the pressure drops during the climb, switch the turbine off automatic and readjust the boost pressure manually. 4) If the lubricant temperature rises above 95°C, the radiator II (in the left wing) should be opened. 5) After reaching peak altitude for the flight concerned, fly horizontally for as long as possible with constant engine power. 6) In the upcoming flights, the pressure ventilation of the cabin is to be switched on in heights above 3km."

The latest known document from Blohm & Voss concerning the BV 155 is a note from April 3 regarding the auxiliary rudder positioning of the BV 155 V2[16].

Beyond that, the flight logbook of Luftwaffe pilot Kurt Reuth[17], who was attached to Blohm & Voss for making ferry flights, contains an entry for April 23, 1945 – Reuth's 1392nd flight – showing that he set off from Neumünster, north of Hamburg, in the BV 155 V1, Werk-Nr. 360051, at 8.50am. After just five minutes, he came down again at nearby Klein Kummerfeld airfield with the note that he had made a 'bruch landung' or 'crash landing'.

If the BV 155 testing programme had continued up to this point it had now been brought to its final conclusion, with Blohm & Voss's Hamburg headquarters being captured by the British 10 days later. What became of the damaged V1 is unknown but presumably Reuth's crash came about as a result of the landing gear failure mentioned by Vogt when he was questioned by the Americans Shuping, Worley and Depew on June 9.

BV 155 ABROAD

The BV 155 V2's various component parts were shipped across to Britain on July 31, 1945, long after the CIOS team's return to London. It was roughly assembled in time to appear as a static exhibit at the German Aircraft Exhibition at Farnborough, arranged by the Royal Aircraft Establishment, from October 29 to November 9, 1945. The catalogue

ABOVE: Unassembled wing components for the BV 155 B V2.

ABOVE: A view of the BV 155 C mockup at Finkenwärder, showing the tail assembly which was similar to if not the same as that of the BV 155 B.

ABOVE: Side-on view of the BV 155 C mockup with the deep chin intake visible to the left. The radiator-less wings are also clearly in evidence.

ABOVE: A somewhat indistinct view of the BV 155 C fuselage framework which was under construction when the war ended.

produced to accompany the exhibition[18] gave a very brief description of the aircraft under 'remarks', stating: "The steel pressure cabin forms part of the structure; there is a three stage supercharger, two stages being exhaust driven in series and one mechanically driven from the engine. It has not been flown in England."

The aircraft was shown as part of 'A Group' and was housed within a hangar opposite He 162 A-2 Werk-Nr. 120097, formerly 'White 3' of JG 1, and Me 163 B Werk-Nr. 191912, which was one of a batch of 24 examples captured by the British. Along with a Bf 109 G and a Fw 190 A, the BV 155 V1 had been 'exploded' to show aileron actuation and the exhaust turbine supercharger. The exhibition catalogue enthused: "The aileron control on this aircraft is unusual in that part of the control is operated by a servo-tab; that is, the stick is connected directly to the tab and the control itself floats freely, being moved by the air forces generated by the tab.

"The whole aileron is split into two portions; the larger inboard portion being operated by the servo-tabs and the outboard portions being connected directly to the stick. The purpose of the outboard section is to give feel directly to the stick, the servo-tabs themselves being aerodynamically balanced and needing therefore little operating force.

"The heaviness of the outboard portion, which is well balanced aerodynamically, is adjusted by cutting off the required amount of the attached tab. The whole control is very light in operation at all speeds."

Two weeks after at the end of the exhibition the V2, now disassembled once again, was transferred to 47 Maintenance Unit at RAF Sealand, Flintshire, arriving on November 26. Two months after that, on January 27, 1946 the aircraft was loaded onto the SS *Port Fairy* and shipped to New York, USA[19]. It finally arrived at Wright Field, Ohio, in August 1946 where it was given the Foreign Equipment number FE-505, later T2-505, before being sent to the Foreign Evaluation Center, Technical Service Command, at Freeman Field, Indiana, where it was evaluated before being sent for storage at Park Ridge, Illinois – arriving there on August 21, 1946.

ABOVE: The fuselage of the BV 155 B V2 after it was brought to Farnborough in Hampshire, UK – presumably before it was assembled and put on display.

ABOVE: The assembled BV 155 B V2 as it appeared as a static exhibit at the German Aircraft Exhibition in Farnborough from October 29 to November 9, 1945. The wingtip of He 162 A-2 Werk-Nr. 120097 is visible just above the man's head.

Around two months later, the RAE's D B Cobb produced a detailed technical report on its features, F A Tech Note No. 257/1 of November 1946[20].

Just over three years after that, with the outbreak of the Korean War, the US government decided that it needed the Park Ridge facility – a dormant factory – to produce aircraft again and ordered the Smithsonian to clear it out. The BV 155 V2 was among 100 aircraft transferred to a federally-owned field at Suitland, Maryland, before the deadline set for removals expired and all remaining aircraft at Park Ridge were scrapped.

Some 26 years later, in 1976, funding was found for a proper storage site comprising 32 buildings and since then the V2 has resided at Silver Hill, Maryland, now known as the Paul E Garber Facility. ●

ABOVE: Another view of the BV 155 B V2 during the German Aircraft Exhibition.

ABOVE: When on display at Farnborough, the BV 155 B V2 shared a hall with a variety of other captured German aircraft. In this view it can be seen behind Me 163 B Werk-Nr. 191912.

ABOVE: The Blohm & Voss BV 155 B V2 – the only surviving BV 155 airframe – photographed at the Smithsonian National Air and Space Museum's Paul E Garber Facility in October 2019. *Photo courtesy of NASM TMS A19600314000CP02*

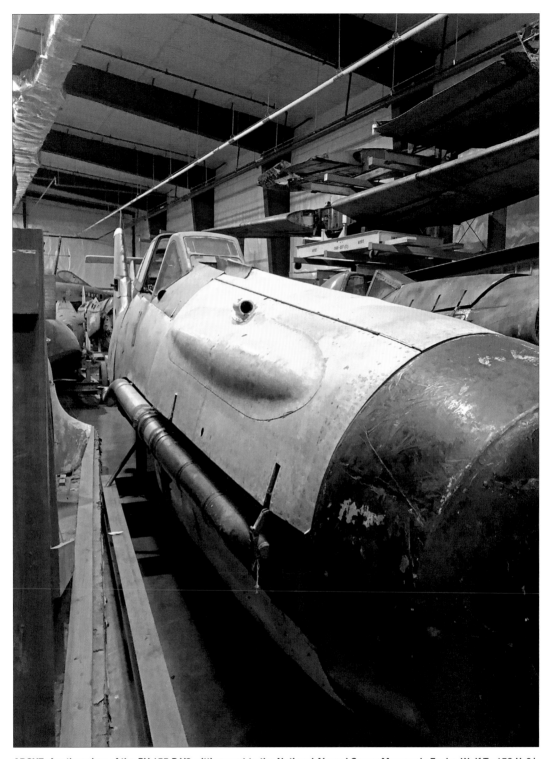

ABOVE: Another view of the BV 155 B V2, sitting next to the National Air and Space Museum's Focke-Wulf Ta 152 H-0/R11. The Ta 152 H was never a competitor for the BV 155, having been designed to operate at lower altitudes.
Photo courtesy of NASM TMS A19600314000CP03

Summary

Throughout 1941 German intelligence had been able to keep a close eye on developments within the US aviation industry through the pages of American magazines and newspapers – which seem to have had no qualms about printing sensitive details that other countries might have worked very hard to keep secret.

Among many other items, the Auslandsnachrichten des General-Luftzeugmeisters Dienst Nr. 3/41/I (RLM intelligence briefing on other countries' aircraft developments) for September 1, 1941, reported on plans to fit the Consolidated B-24D Liberator with a pressure cabin for high-altitude operations, as revealed in *Model Airplane News* of August 1941. Similarly, an article in *Aviation* of July 1941, cited in the same document, candidly discussed Boeing's efforts to design a three-man pressure cabin for operations above an altitude of 12km – the service ceiling of the latest Bf 109 models.

So when America joined the Second World War on the side of Britain and the Allies in December 1941, there was clear concern that the Luftwaffe might soon find itself facing enemy bombers it had no hope of intercepting. These anxieties prompted the RLM to seek a new high-altitude fighter during the spring of 1942. Messerschmitt and Focke-Wulf had already been working to improve the service ceiling of their standard fighters, because a greater peak altitude offers a natural advantage in air-to-air combat, but the RLM wanted them to go further than simply adding a pressure cabin and extended wings to their existing designs.

Focke-Wulf is another story but Messerschmitt focused on tentative work being carried out in with Daimler-Benz on the new DB 628 engine – a DB 605 with a two-stage supercharger for improved performance at high altitude. DB seems to have been doing most of the work, using a Bf 109 F airframe under the factory designation 'Me 409'.

At the same time efforts were being made to correct what was often seen as the Bf 109's biggest flaw: it's narrow track undercarriage. New wings with Fw 190-style gear that folded inwards became part of the Me 409 design, as did the revised Bf 109 G airframe, and it received the official RLM designation Me 155. It was hoped that it could provide the basis for three new aircraft – a standard fighter in parallel to the Me 309, a high-altitude fighter to combat those American bombers and a carrier-based fighter to replace the old Bf 109 E-based Bf 109 T aboard the *Graf Zeppelin*.

With Messerschmitt already working at maximum capacity on other projects, the Me 409/Me 155 was given to French subcontractor SNCAN to tackle. But SNCAN seems have had little time for this work and the Me 155 was pushed to the back of the queue.

Messerschmitt itself seems to have been similarly and understandably disinterested in the type. There was some profit in the carrier-based version – or so it seemed – until the *Graf Zeppelin* was cancelled but there was little ongoing interest in a high-altitude interceptor after the initial panic about American bombers had subsided. It was easier to do the same job by re-engining the Bf 109 G, providing it with simple rectangular inserts to increase its wingspan and keeping its undercarriage the way it was – as the Bf 109 H. Work on all versions of the Me 155 was stopped in early 1943.

When the Me 309 was cancelled and replaced by the Me 209 as the planned successor to the Bf 109, it became necessary to provide a high-altitude option in the form of the Me 209 H. A key aspect of Messerschmitt's (and indeed most other German aircraft manufacturers') design philosophy by January 1943 was specifying the highest possible proportion of existing components for new types to avoid disrupting supply lines and affecting production output. The Me 209 was therefore heavily based on the Bf 109 G but incorporating a new tail, wings with Me 155-style inwards retracting landing gear and a new engine in the form of the Jumo 213.

The situation changed in May 1943 when the RLM decided that a standard fighter modified to operate at 12km, with a ceiling of around 13km, was insufficient. Both the Bf 109 H and Fw 190 H (Ta 152 H after August 1943) were high-altitude fighters but the RLM needed something able to reach 16km.

During early 1943, the British had started fitting the two-stage supercharged Merlin 61 to their latest reconnaissance machines such as the Spitfire PR Mk.XI and Mosquito IX, putting them out of reach for most German interceptors. And as early as September 1, 1942, a meeting of the RLM's GL-Besprechung had heard that a Spitfire (presumably a Mk.VI) fitted with a pressure cabin had been recovered from Dieppe following the disastrous Operation Jubilee raid on the French coast on August 19, 1942.

It was clear that quite apart from the Americans having yet to make any real impact on the European theatre, the British too were now developing a worrying high-altitude capability. The RLM therefore requested that Messerschmitt investigate possibilities for a 16km peak altitude machine. The company responded with the three-stage P 1091 project – the first stage of which was the latest iteration of the Bf 109 H.

The RLM liked the first and third stages but saw no need for the second and the two surviving projects duly joined the growing queue of projects that Messerschmitt still had no real capacity to work on. The company requested more resources but there were none to be had through conventional channels so Generalfeldmarschall Erhard Milch took the radical steps of scrapping production of Blohm & Voss's trio of seaplanes – the BV 138, 222 and 238 – and giving that company's design and production capacity to Messerschmitt. This was arguably a sensible move since the talented team at Blohm & Voss were wasted on continuing to support machines which were largely unnecessary for the Luftwaffe by this point.

Messerschmitt could have chosen to give B&V any of its work – aspects of the Me 262, work on the Me 410, further development of the Me 163, the still-viable Me 209 or even the Me 264 bomber but instead the company handed Blohm & Voss the P 1091 Stage 3. The agreement was signed and the project was given the official designation Me 155 B on September 9, 1943 – there never having been an 'A'. This followed a familiar pattern at Messerschmitt, where the 'A' did not exist until there was a 'B'. Neither the Me 163 nor the Me 328 existed as an 'A' until the Me 163 B and Me 328 B received those official designations – whereupon the earlier prototypes and projects were retrospectively termed Me 163 A and Me 328 A.

While the relationship between Messerschmitt and Blohm & Voss started out well enough, the B&V team seem to have had little conception of what a huge operation Messerschmitt AG was nor how little time the company had to babysit them through the early stages of the project. There was a huge falling out, memorably recalled by Hermann Pohlmann in Thomas H. Hitchcock's Monogram Close-Up 20 Blohm & Voss 155, Monogram 1990, where the Blohm & Voss team were offended and upset because the venue of a meeting was changed at the last minute and they went to the wrong place.

This mix-up resulted in B&V complaining rather petulantly to the RLM, who complained to Messerschmitt, and the two companies' relationship was soon in tatters. The partnership was broken in February 1944 and the aircraft type received Blohm & Voss's company initials: BV 155 B. B&V struggled to get the manpower needed to build the five BV 155 B prototypes ordered because the type's RLM priority rating was set too low. It did, however, find the time to redesign its radiators, making the prototypes obsolete before they were even built.

As 1944 wore on, the Allies' bombing of Germany reached fever pitch and stopping the bomber streams became the Luftwaffe's top priority. This seems to have once again turned the spotlight on the 8-155 and its priority was evidently increased, with an order being placed for 30 examples of the new BV 155 C. By now though it was far too late. The first prototype BV 155 B made only a handful of flights before crashing with a Luftwaffe pilot at the controls. The second prototype was, of course, captured.

It was an incredible feat for the small and under-resourced Blohm & Voss team to design and build a new and complex fighter in around 18 months – but there is no getting away from the fact that those greatly feared high-altitude American bombers never did appear in the skies over Germany. Had it somehow been rushed into production sooner though, the BV 155 might well have made itself useful in combating the latest high-flying Allied reconnaissance aircraft. The Griffon-engined Spitfire PR Mk.XIX had a ceiling of just over 15km, making it almost completely unassailable from the point at which it reached operational units in May 1944 to the end of the war. With BV 155 Cs in Luftwaffe service, the unarmed PR Mk.XIX would have become highly vulnerable.

Acknowledgements

This book would not exist without Ronnie Olsthoorn. It was his idea that I should write it and his boundless enthusiasm for the BV 155 has been an inspiration. Furthermore, without the unwavering support of Stephen Walton at the Imperial War Museum and my friend and fellow primary source research devotee Steve Coates this book would not have been possible. I cannot thank either of them enough. I must also thank Alex Spencer, David Schwartz, Elizabeth Borja, Michael Hankins and Kate Igoe at the National Air and Space Museum for their invaluable aid, and Oliver Thiele, Martin Handig, Gary Webster, J Richard Smith and Calum Douglas for helping to fill in some of the blanks.

Sources

This book has been based entirely on sources produced either during or immediately after the Second World War. Nearly all of the captured German documents that were used as sources may be found on the ADIK, ADRC/MAP and ADRC/T-2 microfilm reels – copies of which are kept at the Smithsonian National Air and Space Museum in Washington, D.C.

The most important reels consulted were 2111, 2119, 2120, 4000 and 5042, but many more reels also contain calculations, reports, technical data, correspondence and other documents relating to the Me 155/ BV 155. These include 156, 158, 225, 228, 229, 230, 231, 235, 239, 2020, 2025, 2080, 2084, 2094, 2103, 2115, 2118, 2121, 2144, 2190, 2211, 2220, 2279, 2337, 2389, 2392, 2395, 2396, 2418, 2404, 2405, 2413, 2415, 2418, 2423, 2432, 2433, 2434, 2443, 2444, 2445, 2446, 2447, 2455, 2456, 2459, 2460, 2464, 2467, 2469, 2472, 2479, 2480, 2481, 2483, 2486, 2488, 2490, 2495, 2605, 2629, 2653, 2664, 2681, 2715, 2771, 2779, 2835, 2868, 2899, 3452, 4001, 4006, 4064, 4075, 4088, 4094, 4095, 4098, 5008, 5010, 5012, 5029 and 5035.

Documents at the National Archives in London:

AIR 40/122 Blohm & Voss photographs
AIR 40/139 Blohm & Voss BV 155
AIR 40/3129 German Aircraft: New and Projected Types by H. F. King 1946
AVIA 6/9241 Royal Aircraft Establishment Technical Note No. F. A. 257/1 Foreign Aircraft – Blohm & Voss 155.B. General Examination by D.B. Cobb 1946

A note on the 'Karawanken' name

No contemporary document has yet surfaced to suggest that the BV 155 had any other designation or code-name in common usage – although Blohm & Voss itself did occasionally and inexplicably refer to it as the 'B 15'. It has been postulated that the code-name 'Karawanken' was used for the aircraft – after the Karawanks mountain range – but again no evidence for this has been found except for a mention of the name on around a dozen postwar file cards prepared in connection with the ADIK, ADRC/MAP and ADRC-T-2 microfilm reels. None of the files to which those cards referred used the name.

It cannot be said for certain that the name 'Karawanken' was never used in connection with the BV 155, but it was most definitely not in regular contemporary usage.

Bibliography

Monogram Close-Up 20 Blohm & Voss 155 by Thomas H. Hitchcock, Monogram Aviation Publications 1990
The Vanishing Paperclips – America's Aerospace Secret, A Personal Account by Hams H. Amtmann, Monogram Aviation Publications 1988
Weltumspannende Memoiren eines Flugzeug-Konstrukteurs by Richard Vogt, Luftfahrt-Verlag Walter Zuerl 1976
Chronik eines Flugzeugwerkes 1932-1945 by H. Pohlmann, Motorbuch Verlag 1979
Warplanes of the Third Reich by William Green, Galahad Books 1970
German Aircraft of the Second World War by J. Richard Smith and Anthony L. Kay, Putnam & Company 1978
The Ultimate Piston Fighters of the Luftwaffe by Justo Miranda, Fonthill Media 2014
Messerschmitt Bf 109 T – The Luftwaffe's Naval Fighter by Marek J. Murawski, Kagero 2010
Luftwaffe Secret Projects: Fighters 1939-1945 by Walter Schick and Ingolf Meyer, Midland Publishing 1997

Notes

Chapter 1: Introduction

1. CIOS report XXV-53 German Aircraft Industry Bremen-Hamburg Area, June 26, 1945
2. IWM Milch Vol. 14/429 GL-Besprechung May 12, 1942 at Rechlin

Chapter 2: Origins

1. DB-2MA-370, Daimler-AG Corporate Archives, Germany
2. IWM FD4355/45 Vol. 4/853 Messerschmitt Aktennotiz Betrifft: Arbeit für Franzosen, March 20, 1942
3. ADIK 4064/1 Messerschmitt report III/165/43 Me 109 H Lebenslauf, August 8, 1943
4. CIOS report IV-7 & V-16 Aircraft – Paris Zone, September 7, 1944
5. ADRC/MAP 5042/79 Der Reichsminister der Luftfahrt St/GL/C-E 2/Festigkeitsprüfstelle Nr. 313/42 geh. Vorläufige Festigkeitsvorschriften Me 409 Fahrwerk, June 25, 1942
6. IWM GDC 15/1020 Messerschmitt Me 155 Festigkeitsvorschriften, July 22, 1942
7. ADIK 158/312 RLM Entwicklungsbesprechung, October 9, 1942
8. ADIK 155/246 Erprobungsstelle Tarnewitz Aktenvermerk des. Dipl. Ing. Fach zur Fa. Mtt,. Augsburg und Leipheim, November 3, 1942
9. IWM GDC 15/275 Messerschmitt Me 155 Vorbemerkung zum Datenblatt, November 13, 1942
10. ADIK 158/318 RLM Entwicklungsbesprechung, September 11, 1942
11. ADRC/T-2 2220/484 Messerschmitt Kurzbaubeschreibungen Me 155 u. Me 309 mit Bo., November 24, 1942
12. IWM Milch Vol. 35/2822 RLM E-Besprechung, January 19, 1943
13. ADRC/MAP 5042/62 Messerschmitt Kobü-Paris Me 155/Allgemein am 26.11.42 in Paris, November 30, 1942
14. ADIK 155/224 Erprobungsstelle Tarnewitz Aktenvermerk Betrifft: Dienstreise des Fl. Ob. Ing. Karsten vom 1. bis 3.12.42 nach Berlin, December 5, 1942
15. ADIK 158/248 RLM Entwicklungsbesprechung, January 8, 1943
16. ADRC/MAP 5039/440 Messerschmitt report A/IV/14/43 Vergleich Me 209-309, January 15, 1943
17. ADIK 158/235 RLM Entwicklungbesprechung, January 21, 1943
18. IWM FD4355/45 Vol. 4/706 Messerschmitt Fernschreiben Berliner Büro – Herrn Urban, February 19, 1943
19. IWM FD4355/45 Vol. 4/703 Messerschmitt Herrn Sindern – PB. Ihre Mitteilung an ZA-H – Betreuung der Kobüe der Firma S.N.C.A.N. und Avions Caudron, February 20, 1943
20. ADRC/MAP 5039/30 RLM Protokoll Festigkeitsvorschriften Me 209, March 5, 1943
21. ADRC/MAP 5039/687 Messerschmitt report III/86/43 Me 209 Höhenjäger Kurzbeschreibung (Zeichnung III/447), April 13, 1943

Chapter 3: Blohm & Voss to the rescue

1. ADRC/MAP 5042/282 Messerschmitt Probü Mitteilung Nr. III/92/43 Me 209 Höhenjäger, May 5, 1943
2. ADRC/MAP 5042/277 Messerschmitt Probü Mitteilung Nr. III/95/43 Höhenflugzeug P 1091: Kühlerdimensionierung, May 11, 1943
3. ADRC/MAP 5042/276 Messerschmitt Probü Mitteilung Nr. III/101/43 Höhenflugzeug mit DB 603 A + TK 11 Kühlerdimensionierung, May 12, 1943
4. ADRC/MAP 5042/275 Messerschmitt Probü Aktennotiz Höhenjäger mit DB 627, May 18, 1943
5. ADRC/MAP 5042/274 Messerschmitt Probü Mitteilung Nr. III/118/43 Fraulein Spangler, May 25, 1943
6. ADRC/MAP 5042/273 Messerschmitt Probü Akten-Vermerk DB 603 mit TKL 15 Telefonische Rücksprache mit Hr. Dr. Bendele, Fa. Hirth-Mot. Stuttg., June 11, 1943
7. ADIK 158/873 RLM Entwicklungbesprechung, June 11, 1943
8. ADIK 158/860 RLM Entwicklungbesprechung, June 15, 1943
9. ADRC/MAP 5042/272 Messerschmitt Probü Mitteilung Nr. III/131/43, June 18, 1943
10. ADRC/MAP 5042/271 Meflug Augsburg Meflug Rechlin Nr. 3696, June 24, 1943
11. ADIK 158/851 RLM Entwicklungbesprechung, June 25, 1943
12. ADRC/T-2 2604/16 Messerschmitt Kurzbeschreibung P 1091 Höhenjäger mit TK 15, June 26, 1943
13. IWM Milch Vol. 21/5673 RLM GL-Besprechung, June 29, 1943
14. IWM GDC 15/650 Messerschmitt Vorschlag einer Höhenjägerentwicklung auf der Basis Me 109/209, July 26, 1943

15 ADIK 4064/1 Messerschmitt report III/165/43 Me 109 H Lebenslauf, August 8, 1943

16 IWM Milch Vol. 23/6488 RLM GL-Besprechung, August 3, 1943

17 IWM Milch Vol. 24/7303 RLM GL-Besprechung, August 13, 1943

18 IWM FD4355/45 Vol. 4/488 Messerschmitt Pohlmann Fernschreiben Herrn Dr. Vogt, August 19, 1943

19 ADRC/MAP 5042/74 Messerschmitt Probü Mitteilung Nr. 84/43 Unterlagen 109 H für Blohm und Voss, August 23, 1943

20 ADRC/MAP 5042/76 Messerschmitt S-Anweisung Nr. 155/001/002 Höhenjäger Me 155 B (Mtt. Projektstufe III) Entwicklung, September 7, 1943

Chapter 4: Split with Messerschmitt

1 ADRC/MAP 5042/54 Messerschmitt Probü Mitteilung Nr. III/173/43 Druck-kabine für Höhenjäger Me 155 B, September 10, 1943

2 ADRC/MAP 5042/36 Meflug Augsburg Blohmwerft Hamburg FS-Nr. 6011 Verbindungstelle Blohm & Voss, September 22, 1943

3 ADRC/MAP 5042/72 Messerschmitt Probü FS an Blohmwerft Hamburg, z. Hd. Herrn Dr Vogt Betr. Ihr FS v. 22.9.43 Nr. 6011, September 23, 1943

4 ADRC/MAP 5042/55-56 Blohm & Voss letter to Messerschmitt Probü, October 5, 1943

5 ADRC/MAP 5042/69 Messerschmitt Probü Mitteilung Nr. III/183/43, October 12, 1943

6 ADRC/MAP 5042/67 Messerschmitt letter to Daimler-Benz TR/56/43, October 19, 1943

7 ADRC/MAP 5042/40 Messerschmitt Probü Mitteilung Nr. III/193/43, October 20, 1943

8 ADRC/MAP 5042/46 Messerschmitt Probü Mitteilung Nr. III/194/43, October 20, 1943

9 ADRC/MAP 5042/35 Messerschmitt Probü Mitteilung Nr. III/196/43, October 20, 1943

10 ADRC/MAP 5042/39 Messerschmitt Probü Mitteilung Nr. III/200/43, October 25, 1943

11 ADRC/MAP 5042/48 Fa. Blohm & Voss, Hamburg – E'BAL d. RLM b. Fa. Blohm & Voss Hamburg, nachrichtl. Fa. Messerschmitt AG, Augsburg, Bericht d.E'BAL am 17.11.43

12 ADRC/T-2 2737/587 Daimler-Benz Höhenjäger Me 155 bei Blohm & Voss, Hamburg (Besuch bei Bl. & Voss am 26.10.43 auf Anforderung von O.I. Schmidt), October 30, 1943

13 ADRC/MAP 5042/64 Messerschmitt Probü Aktennotiz Betrifft: Besprechung Me 155 B; Aufstellung von Diskussionspunkten, November 11, 1943

14 ADRC/MAP 5042/50 Meflug Augsburg Reichsluft Berlin, Fa. Blohm & Voss, Hamburg – E'Bal d. RLM b. Fa. Blohm & Voss, Hamburg, nachr. Fa. Messerschmitt AG, November 24, 1943

15 ADRC/MAP 5042/51 Meflug Augsburg Reichsluft Berlin, Fa. Blohm & Voss, Hamburg – E'Bal d. RLM b. Fa. Blohm & Voss, Hamburg, nachr. Fa. Messerschmitt AG, November 24, 1943

16 ADRC/MAP 5042/60 Messerschmitt Probü Akten-Vermerk Betrifft: Bearbeitung der Me 155 im Projektbüro, November 24, 1943

17 ADRC/T-2 2438/632 Blohm & Voss an den Herrn Reichsminister der Luftfahrt und Oberbefehlshaber der Luftwaffe – GL/C-E 2 Betrifft: Gleitjäger, November 29, 1943

18 ADRC/T-2 2438/638 Reichsminister der Luftfahrt und Oberbefehlshaber der Luftwaffe – GL/C-E 2 letter to Herrn Dr Vogt, Blohm & Voss, August 19, 1943

19 ADIK 4000/120 Blohm & Voss Niederschrift Konstruktionsbesprechung Me 155 B-1, November 29, 1943

20 IWM FD4355/45 Vol. 4/290 Messerschmitt Herrn Dir. Kokothaki – Herrn Bley ZA-H, Zusammenarbeit mit Blohm und Voss, December 1, 1943

21 ADRC/MAP 5042/52 Messerschmitt Probü Mitteilung Nr. III/226/43, December 3, 1943

22 ADIK 4000/118 Blohm & Voss Konstruktionsbesprechung Me 155 B, December 7, 1943

23 WM FD4355/45 Vol. 4/284 Messerschmitt Mitteilung an ZA-H Me 109 H Serienriefmachung, December 8, 1943

24 ADIK 4000/116 Blohm & Voss 3. Konstruktionsbesprechung Me 155 B-1, December 13, 1943

25 ADRC/MAP 5042/75 RLM Technisches Amt Az. 65/44 GL/C-E I T No. 0001/44 geh., January 15, 1944

26 ADIK 4000/114 Blohm & Voss 4. Konstruktionsbesprechung Me 155 B-1, December 20, 1943

27 ADRC/MAP 5039/448 Messerschmitt document A/IV/283/43 Me 209 H Vorbemerkung zum Datenblatt, October 25, 1943

28 ADIK 158/68 RLM Entwicklungsbesprechung, October 29, 1943

29 ADRC/MAP 5039/670 Messerschmitt Mitteilung Nr. III/219/43 Me 209 mit Jumo 213 E (Einheitstriebw.) Kurzbeschreibung (Zeichnung III/539), November 29, 1943

30 ADRC/MAP 5039/683 Messerschmitt Mitteilung Nr. III/220/43 Me 209 mit Jumo 213 E (Einheitstriebwerk) Kurzbeschreibung

(Zeichnung III/548), November 29, 1943

[31] IWM GDC 15/606 Blohm & Voss Höhenjäger für 15 bis 16km Arbeitshöhe mit Triebwerk DB 603 und Turbolader TK 15, January 1944

[32] ADIK 4000/113 Blohm & Voss 5. Konstruktionsbesprechung Me 155 B-1, January 4, 1944

[33] ADIK 4000/112 Blohm & Voss 6. Konstruktionsbesprechung Me 155 B-1, January 10, 1944

[34] ADRC/MAP 5042/75 RLM Technisches Amt Az. 65/44 GL/C-E I T No. 0001/44 geh., January 15, 1944

[35] IWM Milch Vol. 32/971 RLM Besprechung bei der Firma Messerschmitt in Lechfeld, January 20, 1944

[36] ADIK 4000/110 Blohm & Voss Konstruktionsbesprechung Me 155 B, February 3, 1944

[37] ADIK 4000/109 Blohm & Voss Konstruktionsbesprechung Me 155 B, February 5, 1944

[38] ADIK 4000/108 Blohm & Voss Konstruktionsbesprechung BV 155, February 10, 1944

Chapter 5: Back from the brink

[1] ADIK 4000/102 Blohm & Voss Konstruktionsbesprechung BV 155, February 15, 1944

[2] ADIK 4000/107 Blohm & Voss Konstruktionsbesprechung BV 155 am 21.2, February 26, 1944

[3] ADIK 4000/101 Blohm & Voss Konstruktions-Besprechung BV 155, March 9, 1944

[4] ADIK 4000/105 Blohm & Voss Konstruktions-Besprechung BV 155, March 10, 1944

[5] ADIK 4000/103 Blohm & Voss Konstruktions-Besprechung BV 155, March 11, 1944

[6] ADIK 4000/100 Blohm & Voss Konstruktions-Besprechung BV 155, March 14, 1944

[7] ADIK 156/627 RLM Entwicklungsbesprechung, March 17, 1944

[8] ADIK 4000/98 Blohm & Voss Konstruktions-Besprechung am 20.3.44 BV 155, March 21, 1944

[9] IWM Milch Vol. 29/9500 RLM GL-Besprechung, April 7, 1944

[10] ADRC/T-2 2120/75 Blohm & Voss Mitteilung 3b für die Festigkeitsrechnung des Baumusters BV 155 Flugzeugübersichtszeichnung 8-155.00-12 vom 19.4.44, May 18, 1944

[11] ADRC/T-2 2120/8 Blohm & Voss Konstruktions-Besprechung BV 155 + BV 40 am 24. April 1944, April 25, 1944

[12] IWM Milch Vol. 29/9402 RLM GL-Besprechung, April 28, 1944

[13] ADRC/MAP 5035/76 Rechlin Wochenbericht für die Zeit vom 11. bis 17.6.1944, June 17, 1944

[14] ADRC/T-2 2119/937 Gesprächsnotis anlässlich des Besuches von Herrn Bott der E'Stelle Rechlin E 5 VII, July 1, 1944

[15] ADRC/MAP 5035/10 Rechlin Wochenbericht für die Zeit vom 2. bis 8.7.1944, July 8, 1944

[16] IWM Milch Vol. 11/6026 Der Reichsminister für Rüstung und Kriegsproduktion Jägerstab Schnellbericht, July 9, 1944

[17] ADRC/T-2 2111/735 Daimler-Benz Niederschrift Nr. 5073 Besprechung am 12.u.13.7.44 über BV 155 mit DB 603 U und TKL 15, July 18, 1944

[18] ADRC/MAP 5035/22 Rechlin Wochenbericht für die Zeit vom 9. – 15.7.1944, July 15, 1944

[19] ADRC/MAP 5035/36 Rechlin Wochenbericht für die Zeit vom 16. – 22.7.1944, July 22, 1944

[20] ADIK 4000/169 Blohm & Voss Flugleistungen BV 155 – P 205, July 25, 1944

[21] ADIK 4000/123 Blohm & Voss note, July 27, 1944

[22] ADRC/T-2 2119/933 Blohm & Voss Verbindungsstelle bei Messerschmitt AG z. Hd. Herrn Bahlke, July 31, 1944

[23] ADIK 4000/159 Blohm & Voss Rechnungsgewichte BV 155 C, August 2, 1944

[24] ADRC/T-2 2119/930 Blohm & Voss Aktenvermerk Fm A 179 Einbau eines Katapultsitzes in die BV 155 V5 Besprechung in Rechlin am 29.8.1944, August 31, 1944

[25] ADRC/T-2 2111/565 Blohm & Voss Besprechungsnotiz Besprechung über Kühlanlage BV 155 C am 12.9.44, September 13, 1944

[26] J. Richard Smith Collection ref. A2242

[27] ADRC/MAP 5032/56 Chef der Techn. Luftrüstung Nr. 3409/44 g.Kdo., September 15, 1944

[28] ADRC/T-2 2119/922 Blohm & Voss Aktenvermerk FM A-183 Einbau eines Katapultsitzes in BV 155-V5 Übergabe an des Kobü, September 25, 1944

[29] ADIK 4000/90 Blohm & Voss Mitteilung FM-M 357 Triebwerksmesseinbau BV 155 – V1, September 25, 1944

[30] ADIK 4000/94 Blohm & Voss Betriebs-Mitteilung Änderung von Aufträgen für Querrudersteuerung, B-15, September 28, 1944

[31] ADIK 4000/82 Blohm & Voss Protokoll Nr. 532/155/7 Attrappenbesichtigung Triebwerk BV 155 B, October 2, 1944

[32] IWM FD5562/45 Blohm & Voss Flugzeugbau Zentral-Planung Programm – Vorschlag vom 10.10.44

[33] ADIK 4000/86 Blohm & Voss Aktenvermerk FM A-186 Munitionsraumbeheizung BV 155 C, October 12, 1944

[34] ADIK 4000/7 Blohm & Voss Mitteilung Nr. FM M-376 Arbeitsumfang für Funktionserprobung und Standschwingungs-Versuch

BV 155-V1, November 4, 1944

[35] IWM GDC 23/33 British Intelligence Objectives Sub-Committee Group II Halstead Exploiting Centre Translation, Why Produce the Otto Fighter? by Richard Vogt, November 8, 1944

[36] German Aircraft: New and Projected Types A.I.2 (g) Report No. 2383 by H. F. King January 1946

[37] ADRC/MAP 5026/484 OKL Chef der Technischen Luftrüstung Fl.E Nr. 33580/44 geh. (E 6 IV), December 6, 1944

[38] ADIK 4000/23 Blohm & Voss Mitteilung Nr. FM M-394, January 3, 1945

[39] ADIK 4000/48 Blohm & Voss Protokoll Nr. 534/155/9 Attrappenbesichtigung 8-155 C, January 15-16, 1945

[40] ADRC/MAP 5026/483 RLM TLR-Fl.E/W 1 IV Az. 72 d 50 Nr. 45195/45 geh., January 22, 1945

Chapter 6: The beginning and the end

[1] ADIK 4000/57 Blohm & Voss Endbeanstandungen der Masch. B 15, V 1, January 31, 1945

[2] ADIK 4000/31 OKL, Chef TLR F1 – E2 FP und B.u.V. Aktenvermerk FM A-192 BV 155-B V1 Flattersicherheit, February 5, 1945

[3] ADIK 4000/29 Blohm & Voss Bericht über den ersten Flug mit BV 155 – V 1 Werk-Nr. 360051 am 8.2.1945, February 8, 1945

[4] ADIK 4000/24 Blohm & Voss note Betr.: B 15 V 4 – Versichsflugzeug für Flugschwingungsversuche, February 9, 1945

[5] ADIK 4000/27 Blohm & Voss Flugbericht 2. Flug mit BV 155 – V1, W.Nr. 360051 am 10.2.1945, February 14, 1945

[6] KTB der Chef TLR Berichtswoche 5.2/11.2.1945 via http://cdvandt.org/ktb-chef-tlr.htm

[7] ADIK 4000/43 Blohm & Voss Betriebs-Mitteilung FM M-411 BV 155 C – Luftführung im Kabinendach, February 15, 1945

[8] ADIK 4000/11 Blohm & Voss Mitteilung FM 414 Dritter Flug BV 155, February 19, 1945

[9] ADIK 4000/15 Blohm & Voss Bericht über den 3. Flug der BV 155 V 1 am 28.2.1945, March 3, 1945

[10] ADRC/T-2 8051/132 ZWB 13872 Entwicklungs-Notprogramm

[11] ADIK 4000/10 Blohm & Voss Betriebs-Mitteilung Flugstunden für dringende Erprobungsaufgaben, March 7, 1945

[12] Eckhard Sternberg collection via https://luftwaffe-research-group.org

[13] ADRC/T-2 3282/270 Prof. Dr. Ing. Günther Bock, DVL – Herrn Dipl.-Ing. Wehrse, Focke-Wulf, Fertigungsprogramm und Entwicklungsarbeiten, March 12, 1945

[14] KTB der Chef TLR Berichtswoche 5.3/15.3.1945 via http://cdvandt.org/ktb-chef-tlr.htm

[15] ADIK 4000/20 Blohm & Voss Betriebs-Mitteilung FM M-419, March 20, 1945

[16] ADIK 4000/4 Blohm & Voss Mitteilung Nr. FM M-423, April 3, 1945

[17] Oliver Thiele collection

[18] Oliver Thiele collection ref. D5299

[19] Joe F. Baugher home page http://www.joebaugher.com/usaf_serials/Captured_Axis_Aircraft.html

[20] TNA AVIA 6/9241 Royal Aircraft Establishment Technical Note No. F. A. 257/1 Foreign Aircraft – Blohm and Voss 155.B General Examination by D. B. Cobb B.Sc

Index

Appendix I

Royal Aircraft Establishment
Foreign Aircraft – Blohm und Voss 155.B
General Examination, November 1946

The Royal Aircraft Establishment carried out a highly detailed technical examination of the Blohm & Voss BV 155 B V2 when it was located at Farnborough, Hants. during the autumn of 1945. A report on this study was eventually issued as Technical Note No. F. A. 257/1 in November 1946. The document offers an unparalleled description of aircraft – offering fine detail observations which might otherwise be unknown, such as the fact that the engine cowling was not attached to the fuselage in any way but was mounted entirely onto the engine itself. And the use of rubberised fabric to allow for movement of the engine. This is about as close as it is possible to get to the aircraft without being able to see it in person. The original writing style has been retained throughout.

CONFIDENTIAL

623.746 (43) BLOHM & VOSS 155
F. A. Tech.Note No. 257/1
November, 1946.

ROYAL AIRCRAFT ESTABLISHMENT, FARNBOROUGH

Foreign Aircraft – Blohm and Voss 155.B.
General Examination
by
D.B. Cobb, B.Sc.

INTRODUCTION

The BV.155.B is a single seat, single engined high altitude fighter. It has a maximum speed of 431 m.p.h. between 51,000 and 53,000 feet and a ceiling of 56,000 feet and is armed with 2 x 20 m.m. and 1 x 30 m.m. guns.

The design is believed to be based upon a former Messerschmitt Project which was handed over to Blohm and Voss for development. The outer wings and the rear fuselage are closely reminiscent of the Me.109. The take-off weight with 110 galls. of fuel is 12,320 lb. giving a wing loading of 29.3 lb/sq.ft. The wing span is 67 ft.

The aircraft examined had not been assembled and evidently the manufacture of some parts had never been finished.

POWER PLANT – FIGS. 2-8

The engine is a Daimler Benz 603 U (ref.1). It is a 12 cylinder, direct injection, liquid cooled inverted 'V', using B4 fuel and developing 1430 B.H.P. at 49,000 ft. The TKL.15 exhaust driven supercharger unit is mounted in a fuselage compartment (Fig.5) behind the pilot. The exhaust gases are collected from the manifold on each side of the engine and passed via two spherical joints 1 and one sliding joint 2 (which allow for expansion and the movement of the engine on its mountings) into 5½" dia. ducts 3 passing along the outside of the fuselage through a further flexible connection 4 to the branch on each side leading to the turbine compartment, one branch on each side leading to the turbine the

FIG.1.   B.V. 155

FIG. 2.   B.V. 155

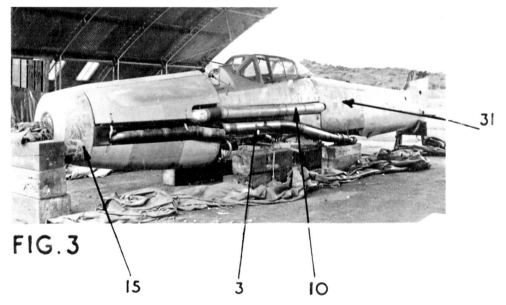

FIG.3

15   3   10

31

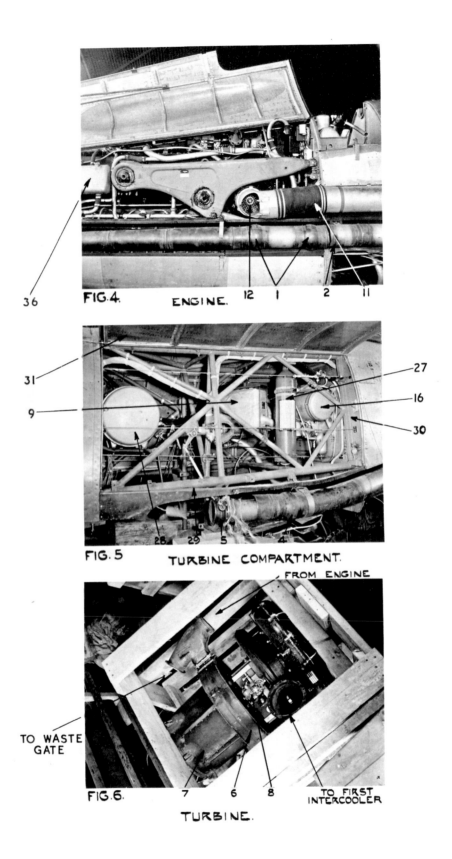

36   FIG.4.   ENGINE.   12 1   2   11

31
9   27
                                           16
                                           30

28 29 5 4

FIG.5   TURBINE COMPARTMENT.

FROM ENGINE

TO WASTE
GATE

FIG.6.   7   6   8   TO FIRST
                        INTERCOOLER

TURBINE.

other branches having waste-gate valves leading to the exhaust duct below the rear fuselage. The waste-gate valves regulate the quantity of gas passing to the turbine and hence control its speed.

The turbine supercharger unit is mounted with its axis in the direction of flight and the exhaust gases pass rearward from the collecting chamber 6 through one row of fixed and one row of moving blades to the exit duct 7. The turbine blades are hollow and are cooled by air drawn in from the air entry duct below the pilot through a separate pipe to the centre of the rotor and passing outward through the blades to escape from their tips into the exhaust exit duct. The supercharger, placed in front of the turbine, is of the two stage centrifugal type and between the supercharger and the turbine is the hydraulic control mechanism 8. Air is drawn into the eye of the first stage from the entry duct below the pilot and from the volute of the second stage it passes to the first intercooler 9. From the intercooler it passed through a pipe 10 on the outside of the fuselage on the port side to the entry of the single stage supercharger driven by the engine, through a hydraulic coupling. A length of rubberised fabric 11 secured by hose clips is used to allow for engine movement and a flap valve 12 with a rubber sealing ring opens automatically to allow air to reach the engine when the exhaust turbine is not working. Air from the engine driven supercharger is then passed through the second intercooler to the inlet manifold situated between the cylinder blocks.

There are two separate coolant systems. The first consists of starboard radiator which cools the engine itself and has two service tanks 36 placed alongside the crankcase. The second system has coolant passing in series through the port radiator, the oil heat exchanger 14 which is placed in front of the centre section spar and the two air heat exchangers and has a service tank placed in the turbine compartment.

The lubricant for the engine is contained in an annular 26½ gallon tank 15 round the nose of the crankcase and that for the turbine in a 4½ gallon tank 16 in the turbine compartment.
Behind each radiator is a large fairing at the bottom of which is a cascade of aerofoil section flaps 40 operated by a thermostatically controlled hydraulic jack, which regulate the air flow through the radiator.

WING – FIGS. 7-13

The wing is made up of three main units. The centre section, which carries the two large radiators and the undercarriage, is attached at four points below the fuselage and each outer wing is attached at three points just outboard of the radiator. The centre section consists in effect of a rectangular steel box spar to which nose and trailing edge portions are attached to make up a wing. The spar which also serves as a fuel tank is in the form of a box which has the same depth over its whole span but varies in chordwise dimension from 1'-9" below the fuselage to 8" at the root of the outer wing. It is made in upper and lower halve welded together along the centre line. Four spanwise hat sections are welded onto the inside of the box at the top and bottom and it is further reinforced by diaphragms welded into place. The box is made up of 5 m.m. thick plain carbon steel plate with an ultimate tensile strength of 31 ton/sq.in. All the loads are carried by the spar and accordingly the skin is very thin (0.035" over nose portion and 0.024" over trailing portion). The skin is supported by plate ribs between which are chordwise 'Z' section formers at 6" pitch. At its upper and lower edges where the skin abuts on the spar it is riveted to four spanwise stringers of 2" x 1" x 0.68" 'Z' section. Each half rib is secured by bolts 13 top and bottom, 19, attached to the ribs which support the side fairings of the duct. Midway between the fuselage and the radiator is a 20 m.m. MG.151 mounted in a sleeve in the spar, the ammunition being loaded through a large door, 17, in the upper wing skin aft of the spar. The wing is attached to the fuselage by four pins, passing through lugs 18 welded to the spar, the two rear ones being adjustable vertically.

The outer wing appears to correspond very closely with the wing of the Me.109. It is based on a single spar placed at 40% of the chord from the leading edge and the lower surface is composed largely of detachable panels which give access for fabrication and maintenance.

The spar is composed at the root of a plate web with 1½" x 2" angles and 5" x ½" flange plates. The flange plates are machined down towards the tip and one pair of flange angles are discontinued.

There are also front and rear spanwise members. The front member consists at the root of a 9" x 2" channel reinforced with two 1" x 1" angles and the rear one of a 7" x 1½" channel which carries the aileron hinges, and both are tapered in depth towards the tip. There are seven ribs consisting of pressed plates with flanged edges to which the skin is riveted. Between each pair of ribs are chordwise 3" x 1½" x 0.06" 'Z' formers, 20, at 9" pitch. The rib webs are riveted to the webs of the spar and front and rear members which are further supported by lipped angles, 21, at 9" pitch between the ribs. The root rib is further reinforced by heavy angles, 22, riveted to the skin along the upper and lower edges. The skin thickness fore and aft of the spar is 0.08" at the root and 0.05" at the tip. The vertical bending appears to be carried entirely by the spar and the torque to be shared between the 'D' nose and the boxes formed by the spar; front and rear webs and the upper and lower skins. As shown in Fig.11, the large detachable panels in the lower surface are secured by screws and anchor stiff nuts. The wing tip is a separate unit stiffened by internal diaphragms and is attached to the wing by two pins.

The outer wing attached to the centre section by three pins with spherical bushes in steel fittings. Two of the pins are placed on the spar with their axes at right angles to one another and the third on the leading edge member (Fig.9). This leading edge pin transmits vertical loads to the 'V' shaped member 23 consisting of tubes welded to the box spar of the centre section. In this way torsion loads are transferred from the outer wing to the box spar. This wing joint is enclosed by a fairing secured by screws in anchor stiff nuts 24.

FLAPS

The flaps extend in one piece on each side from the fuselage to the radiator. The flap is composed of a 2" diameter, 0.08" light alloy tube 25, a skin plate and pressed ribs riveted to the tube and skin at 7" pitch. The flap is operated by a hydraulic jack placed inside the wing and rotating the tube by means of a bell crank.

The aileron extends in two sections over the whole of the outer wing. The control column is directly connection only with the outer section of each aileron and this is linked to the tab on the inner section in such a way that when the outer section is depressed, the tab is raised so that the inner section is servo operated. The control from the cockpit is by a pair of cables to a tiller 26 made up of steel pressings, thence by a push pull tube and bell cranks to a chordwise disposed shaft on which is a crank which engages by a ball and sliding block joint with a hinged bracket projecting forward from the aileron. The ailerons are metal covered with ribs at 7" pitch and a steel tube forming the spar. They are hinged to welded steel brackets bolted to the trailing edge member of the wing opposite alternate wing ribs. The tab is of plywood construction.

FUSELAGE – FIGS. 2,3,5,14,15 AND 16

The fuselage consists of three parts, the pressure cabin, the turbine compartment and the rear fuselage.

The pressure cabin is made up in the form of a box from welded steel sheets and attachment fittings are welded to it to receive the engine mounting at four points in front, the wing spar at four points underneath and the tubular frame of the turbine compartment at four points behind. At the top is the electrically heated bullet resisting glass windscreen and the sliding sealable canopy. The sides are covered by thin light alloy sheets attached by screws to produce a smooth exterior skin.

Behind the pressure cabin is a section made up from four longerons 29 of 2" diameter steel tubes braced in an irregular lattice form by 1½" diameter tubes welded together as shown in Fig.5. This structure carries the exhaust turbine supercharger and first intercooler and their accessories, a large fire extinguisher 27 and a pressurised container 28 for the electric accumulator. The forward compartment of the section is divided by a bulkhead 30 from the turbine compartment and contains the oxygen bottles (of the 3 sphere steel type), part of the radio equipment and part of the cabin pressurising equipment. The sides and top of this forward compartment and the top of the turbine compartment consist of thin light alloy sheets supported by stiffeners riveted to them and secured to

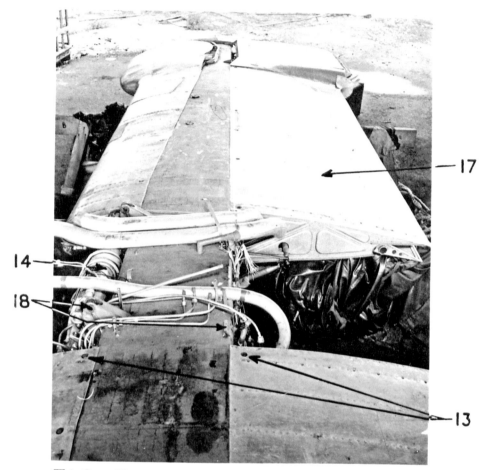

FIG. 7.   WING CENTRE SECTION.

FIG. 8

RADIATOR.

FIG. 10   WING.

FIG. 11   OUTER WING ATTACHMENT.

the tubular steel frame by screws. The sides of the turbine compartment consist of two large doors 31 made up of light alloy panels stiffened by vertical hat sections and hinged along their upper edge to give access to the mechanism inside. Below both these compartments are attached the light alloy duct which leads air into the turbine and the thin steel sheet exhaust channel. At the rear of the turbine compartment is another plate bulkhead, aft of which is the rear fuselage which is of normal monocoque construction and is closely reminiscent of the Me.109.

The rear fuselage is made in two halves joined in two rows of rivets through the crown of an extra wide "top hat" longitudinal stringer at the top and bottom. In addition there are five 2" x 3/4 " "top hat" stringers 32 on each side. The formers are 1'-8" apart and consist of 1½" deep 'Z' sections 33 passing inside the stringers and riveted to them but not to the skin.

TAIL – FIG.16
At the rear of the fuselage is a "stern frame" 34 to which is attached the fin spar, the hinge 37 for the variable incidence tailplane and the tail wheel shock absorber. Forward of this is a lighter inclined frame 35 to which is attached the front member of the fin and the electric jack, by which the leading edge of the tailplane is moved up and down.

The fin is of metal construction and its two "spars" are bolted to the upper ends of the fuselage frames 34 and 35. The tailplane is of plywood construction except for the tips which are light alloy pressings attached by screws. The span is 16'-4". The spar is bolted to the hinge 37 and the nose carries a projecting block which slides up and down between the guides 38 by which it is restrained laterally. This block is attached to the upper end of an electrically operated screw jack placed inside the fuselage and controlled by a switch at the pilot's left hand. Near this switch is an electrical tailplane position indicator.
The rudder and elevators are of metal and of similar construction to the ailerons.
The rudder, elevator and ailerons are controlled by rotating shafts passing through the walls of the pressure cabin. Outside the pressure cabin these shafts carry pressed steel tillers from which extend steel cables. The elevator and rudder are each controlled by a single pair of cables passing down the fuselage to the tail.

UNDERCARRIAGE – FIG.2
The undercarriage is of the tailwheel type, the main wheels having a wide track and retracting outward into the enlarged portions of the wing in front of the radiators. Each main wheel hub is mounted on a single tubular support curved so that the shock absorber cylinder is placed directly above the wheel. The upper end of the shock absorber is attached to the forward end of a shaft which is free to rotate in bearings in a sleeve welded into the spar of the centre section of the wing. The wheel is retracted and extended by a hydraulic jack attached to the wing spar, the wheel housing being closed by flaps operated by a separate jack. The shock absorbers have scissor links to prevent rotation.

The tyres are 840 x 300 and the brakes appear to be of the hydraulically operated two shoe type usual in German fighters.

The tailwheel is mounted in a welded steel fork below and oleo-pneumatic shock absorber. The fork is centred by a cam loaded by the shock absorber and can be locked by a bowden control. The bottom of the shock absorber cylinder is hinged 39 to the stern frame and is retracted by a hydraulic jack attached to its upper end, in the same way as the tailwheel of the Me.109F.

ENGINE MOUNTING – FIG.4
The engine is mounted in four shock absorbing rubber bushes in a pair of welded pressed steel box section bearer which are attached at four points to the front of the steel pressure cabin. The cowling is attached entirely to the engine and not to the fuselage. It consists of three large panels with integral stiffeners secured by toggle fasteners to the exhaust manifolds. The 30 m.m. gun is mounted on the rear of the crankcase and fires through the propeller hub.

FIG. 12   OUTER WING.

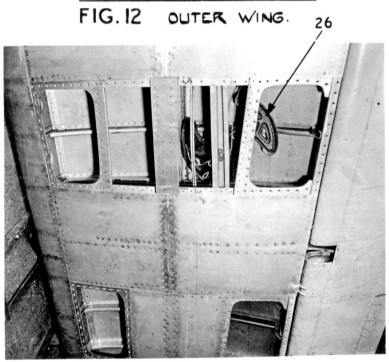

FIG. 13   AILERON

40

B.V. 155

FUEL TANKS

It is believed that the box spar is divided into five tanks. The centre one holds 30 gallons and fuel is pumped from it to the service pump on the engine by a normal electric emersed pump. On each side of the centre tank is one of 51 gallons capacity and outboard of this pair is a further pair each of 66 gallons capacity. Air under pressure from the supercharger is used to force fuel from the outer tanks to the centre one.

EQUIPMENT

The engine starting primer pump and tank of starting fuel are placed on the left side of the instrument panel. The cockpit contains the normal German fighter instruments and in addition, a speed indicator for the turbine, and "equivalent cockpit altitude" indicator. Air for the cabin is taken from the delivery of the turbo compressor and passed to a Knorr compressor driven by the engine and thence through a filter and control valve to the cabin.

REFERENCE

No.   Title, etc.

1   EAM 126   Jan 1944
                 Examination of D.B. 603 engine.

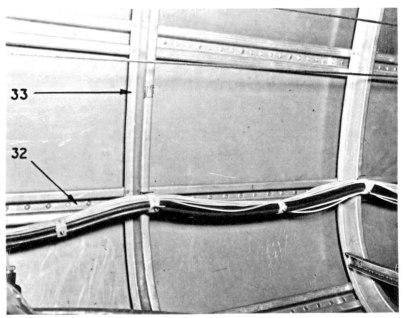

FIG.15   REAR FUSELAGE.

FIG.16   TAIL.

Appendix II

From Messerschmitt P 1091 to Blohm & Voss BV 155 C-1

Type	Date	Wingspan	Wing area	Length	Main Wheel	Tail wheel	Engine	Empty weight	Takeoff weight	Armament
P 1091 Stage 1	July 26, 1943	13.2m	22.2m²	9.02m	660 x 160	350 x 135	DB 605 A + GM 1	2875kg	3540kg	1 x MK 108 with 70 rds + 2 x MG 151/20 with 140 rds
P 1091 Stage 2	July 26, 1943	21m	39m²	n/a	740 x 210	380 x 150	DB 605 A + O2	3724kg	4410kg	1 x MK 108 with 70 rds + 2 x MG 151/20 with 200 rds or 2 x MK 108 with 70 rds
P 1091 Stage 3	July 26, 1943	21m	39m²	n/a	740 x 210	380 x 150	DB 603 A + TKL 15	4672kg	5444kg	1 x MK 108 with 75 rds + 2 x MG 151/20 with 200 rds or 2 x MK 108 with 70 rds
Me 155 B-1 (drwg. 8-155.00-11)	December 28, 1943	20.5m	39m²	12m	840 x 300	380 x 150	DB 603 + TKL 15	4869kg	5521kg	Four options: A) 1 x MK 108 with 60 rds + 2 x MG 151/20 with 200 rds B) 1 x MK 103 with 60 rds + 2 x MG 151/20 with 200 rds C) 1 x MK 108 with 60 rds + 2 x MK 108 with 60 rds D) 1 x MK 103 with 60 rds + 2 x MK 103 with 60 rds
BV 155 B-1 (drwg. 8-155.00-12)	April 19, 1944	20.25m	39m²	12.05m	840 x 300	380 x 150	DB 603 U	n/a	6000kg	1 x MK 108 with 75 rds + 2 x MG 151/20 with 200rds
P 205	circa July 1944	18.65m	36.5m²	12.1m	n/a	n/a	DB 603 U	n/a	6000kg	1 x MK 108 with 75 rds + 2 x MG 151/20 with 200rds
BV 155 B-1	circa August 1944	20.33m	38.5m²	12.1m	840 x 300	380 x 150	DB 603 U	5199kg	5390kg	1 x MK 108 with 75 rds + 2 x MG 151/20 with 200rds
BV 155 C-1	circa August 1944	19.05m	35.8m²	12.1m	840 x 300	380 x 150	DB 603 U	5682kg	6384kg	1 x MK 108 with 75 rds + 2 x MG 151/20 with 200 rds